The Abingdon
Preaching Annual
2024

The Abingdon
Preaching
Annual

2024

Planning Sermons
for Fifty-Two Sundays

Charley Reeb, General Editor

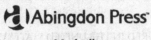

Abingdon Press™

Nashville

THE ABINGDON PREACHING ANNUAL 2024:
PLANNING SERMONS FOR FIFTY-TWO SUNDAYS

Copyright © 2023 by Abingdon Press

ISBN 978-1-7910-2706-3

Scripture quotations unless noted otherwise are from the Common English Bible. Copyright © 2011 by the Common English Bible. All rights reserved. Used by permission. www.CommonEnglishBible.com.

Scripture quotations marked BSB are from The Holy Bible, Berean Study Bible, BSB. Copyright ©2016, 2018 by Bible Hub. Used by Permission. All Rights Reserved Worldwide.

Scripture quotations marked ESV are from the ESV® Bible (The Holy Bible, English Standard Version®), copyright © 2001 by Crossway, a publishing ministry of Good News Publishers. Used by permission. All rights reserved.

Scripture quotations marked KJV are from The Authorized (King James) Version. Rights in the Authorized Version in the United Kingdom are vested in the Crown. Reproduced by permission of the Crown's patentee, Cambridge University Press.

Scripture quotations marked (NIV) are taken from the Holy Bible, New International Version®, NIV®. Copyright © 1973, 1978, 1984, 2011 by Biblica, Inc.™ Used by permission of Zondervan. All rights reserved worldwide. www.zondervan.com. The "NIV" and "New International Version" are trademarks registered in the United States Patent and Trademark Office by Biblica, Inc.™

Scripture quotations marked NRSVUE are from the New Revised Standard Version, Updated Edition. Copyright © 2021 National Council of Churches of Christ in the United States of America. Used by permission. All rights reserved worldwide.

Scripture quotations marked RSV are from the Revised Standard Version of the Bible, copyright © 1946, 1952, and 1971 National Council of the Churches of Christ in the United States of America. Used by permission. All rights reserved worldwide. http://nrsvbibles.org/.

The content for pages 75–83 is taken from *Will Willimon's Pulpit Resource*, available by subscription at www.MinistryMatters.com.

MANUFACTURED IN THE UNITED STATES OF AMERICA

Contents

🖋 = Sunday in Lent   ☻ = Sunday of Advent

Preface

James Earl Massey described the task of preaching as a "burdensome joy." Those of us who are called to preach know all too well the truth of that description. Sundays just keep on coming and there is the relentless question, "Will I have a word this week for my people that is worth the effort they make to skip other desirable Sunday morning options and come to worship?" We pray, toil, worry, and even obsess over each sermon, hoping that our offering will not only be what our listeners need but also acceptable and pleasing to God. What a burden, indeed! Yet, there are those moments when we sense the movement of the Holy Spirit through our preaching, and it is pure joy. Hearts are touched, people are called, decisions of faith are made. God chose to use one of our sermons to make a difference in the lives of our listeners, and it is both humbling and exhilarating. Those events remind us why we embrace this "burdensome joy."

The Abingdon Preaching Annual is a resource dedicated to those who seek to be faithful to the "burdensome joy" of preaching. It helps equip preachers who earnestly desire for their sermons to be used by God to touch the hearts and lives of people. This annual is filled with rich interpretations, keen insights, and prophetic guidance that will empower lectionary preachers to prepare inspiring sermons week after week.

Another valuable resource for preachers is ministrymatters.com. This site contains a wealth of instruction and inspiration for sermons and preaching. Visit the site and explore all the ways you can enhance your preaching ministry and increase your effectiveness in the pulpit.

Many thanks to the gifted team of editors at Abingdon Press for helping to bring this resource to life.

Charley Reeb
General Editor

Sermon Helps

Sermon Helps

January 6, 2024–
Epiphany of the Lord

Isaiah 60:1-6; Psalm 72:1-7, 10-14; Ephesians 3:1-12; **Matthew 2:1-12**

January 7, 2024–
Baptism of the Lord

Genesis 1:1-5; Psalm 29; Acts 19:1-7; **Mark 1:4-11**

Sam Parkes

Preacher to Preacher Prayer

Beautiful Savior, the star-promise of your Nativity has drawn us into an Advent journey to your creche. We beheld your radiance shining from a rude and unexpected manger. And now the feast is done; the culture is ready to "return home" to the ordinary and predictable. As I preach, help me call your people past Bethlehem to the verge of Jordan that we may hear your startling voice in our baptismal memories, "You are my child, whom I dearly love." Amen.

Commentary

This Sunday brings a little bit of "East meets West" in the Revised Common Lectionary, and at first glance it may seem like a lot to cram into a single Sunday! Liturgically, the Feast of the Epiphany functions like a hinge; it is the culmination of the Advent-Christmas-Epiphany cycle through which we have been preparing for Christ's coming and celebrating his Nativity. But the "arrow" of the promise and fulfillment of God's incarnation in Jesus aims toward the theology proclaimed on this day: God *reveals* Godself to humanity in Jesus, and we can *recognize* God in the person of Jesus.

The Epiphany also inaugurates a season of Ordinary Time in which the lessons richly describe that revelation and recognition. While much of our Western culture is enamored with the stories of Christ's birth (and the annual consumerist orgy it has engendered), Christian liturgy moves us on to the revelatory significance of that birth. In the Western church, the visit of the magi has been the signal story of the Epiphany impulse; in the Eastern Church that impulse moves toward the Lord's baptism in the Jordan.

Since Epiphany falls on a Saturday this year, the likelihood that many Protestants will observe the feast is small. However, since this feast is the theological "target" of the cycle, we would be remiss to merely let it pass by. Thus, we invite you to return to the days of the early church when all of these observances collected into a single grand feast. And since it is the first Sunday of the month when many Protestants celebrate the Eucharist, let's prepare for a grand occasion!

The rub comes as the preacher settles in to choose a path for proclamation. Toward what aspect of these rich passages should the sermon draw the hearers? And which texts should be read aloud? I will proceed to offer one potential path for this liturgy and for the sermon in its context.

Usually, I encourage preachers to focus on only one text each week. However, this Sunday you could use both the Matthew 2 passage as well as the Mark 1 passage. In the next section, I will recommend a liturgical approach to using both. For preaching, one might choose the following theme for this sermon: *God delights in the person and ministry of Jesus.* Both texts have been preserved by the church for their epiphanic value and reveal a delightful extravagance poured out before Jesus in the midst of odd, even rude, circumstances of striking intimacy. Further, each episode leads into a difficult journey fraught with trial.

In fulfillment of Numbers 24:17 and Isaiah 60, a divinely appointed star guides a group (Three? Seven? Twenty? The text doesn't say.) of Persian soothsayers to seek out "the newborn king of the Jews" (Matthew 2:2) in Jerusalem. Kings are born in capitals, right? Not this one. After a bit of Bible study, the magi are guided to Bethlehem by King Herod, whose power quakes at the news. It appears that "delight" is not a universal response to this birth. The magi follow the star and arrive not at a palace, but at a common house in a small town. They offer the holy family their extravagant gifts of gold, frankincense, and myrrh right there in the living room of a home that would have been indistinguishable from its neighbors. A simple Google search will tell you what supposed allegorical value these gifts have: gold for royalty, incense for divinity, and myrrh with its "bitter perfume" for anointing the dead, and so forth. However, if we let the Scriptures themselves define the meaning of these gifts, a better interpretation might be found. These three items figure greatly in two biblical "centers": all three items are integral to the details of the tabernacle in the exodus tradition. The tent of meeting is God's design to be near God's children and was a place of much gold, frankincense, and myrrh—extravagant expressions of the covenant love between God and his freshly redeemed nation. These elements also figure in the Song of Songs as visual and olfactory symbols of the intimate joy between lovers. Myrrh is cited more in that book than in any other with nary a whiff of death being referenced. If no one else seems to recognize the revelation of God in this child, God will call Gentile alchemists to do for God what no one else will: offer extravagant love and adornment to his Beloved, the new "tabernacle" where God's glory can be seen . . . if one has eyes to see.

Mark's spartan narrative of Jesus's baptism expresses similar sentiments. Again, where is the Beloved to be encountered? Not in Jerusalem. Rather, he is out at the Jordan responding to the ministry of the unlikely, John the Baptizer, God's rude prophet who, like the magi, can sense the value in the "One stronger than I" who is approaching. In Mark's telling, Jesus's baptism is intimately personal: *He* saw the sky torn and the Spirit-dove descending. *He* heard the voice from heaven proclaiming God's love and happiness. Nothing in the text indicates that anyone else, even John, witnessed this extravagance.

Both narratives are followed by journeys of difficulty and testing; Matthew's Joseph is warned to flee from Herod's jealous blade; Mark's Jesus is driven into the wilderness with wild beasts and the tempting Adversary. In both, angels of extravagance guide and minister to the Beloved. In these narratives, God calls us to see the beauty, worth, and value of the Son shining in the world's rude locales. Of course, we know where these narratives are taking us; our Lenten Journey is mere weeks away. Jesus will descend into an ugly baptism of torture and death. Few will see his worth there outside the city. Will we, with God, recognize the One whose "love is as strong as death, passionate love unrelenting as the grave" (Song of Songs 8:6)?

Bringing the Text to Life

This is a Sunday to cap off the Advent-Christmas-Epiphany cycle with worship on a grand scale that reflects our recognition of Jesus's worth and value to our communities of faith. Let's not allow the pageantry of Christmas Eve/Day and the new year demands to "get back to normal" to temper our enthusiastic expressions of hope, love, joy, and peace in Jesus Christ. All our worship since the first Sunday of Advent has been aimed not *at* the Nativity but *through* it to the target of this moment.

This is the day to extol the exquisite loveliness of the living Christ, particularly as we encounter him in the rude, unexpected, out-of-the-way places of life and ministry. What are the unsung and out-of-the-way places in your life, culture, and church through whom God is revealing beauty, truth, and goodness? Who is it that needs to hear your "voice from heaven" speak words of blessing and love?

In the parish I serve, we have a robust Celebrate Recovery (CR) ministry. Every week, scores of people gather to seek God's help in overcoming their hurts, habits, and hang-ups. Patricia is one of our leaders. Now in her seventies, Pat's commitment to her own recovery and that of others is constant and quiet. Recently one of her sponsees with whom she had worked for years relapsed into her addiction and died from her alcoholism. "Herod" is always seeking to cut hope short and preserve power. As shaken as Patricia was from the news, she was in no way discouraged from her mission to seek out and save those lost in their addictions. Unassumingly and quietly, Pat shows up week after week to shine the star of hope into weary lives: "How could I give up? My sponsee's death shows that CR is more important than ever." Nothing would make me happier as a pastor than to open several treasure chests in her direction. Pat needs to hear, in personal and intimate terms, that she is dearly loved by God. I'm not worthy to loosen her sandal straps. Her life is epiphanic. Let those with eyes to see recognize Christ's life living through hers.

January 14, 2024–Second Sunday after the Epiphany

1 Samuel 3:1-10, (11-20); Psalm 139:1-6, 13-18; **1 Corinthians 6:12-20***;*
John 1:43-51

Sam Parkes

Preacher to Preacher Prayer

Faithful God, in baptism you buried me in Christ Jesus and raised me to a new life of freedom circumscribed by love. Let the temple-body of my congregation be filled with your Holy Spirit. Kindle my bones with such passionate ardor for your Word and these people that a thousand tongues would not suffice to convey the triumphs of your grace. Amen.

Commentary

The Epiphany season assigns texts that concern God's revelation in Jesus Christ to the world and our recognition of what God has revealed. In his missive to the church in Corinth, Paul hangs out his shingle as a licensed marriage and family therapist to help us recognize in our own bodies and spirits what God has done in Jesus: united our spirits with his own. The two (the believer and Christ) have become one flesh.

Corinth was an ethnically and religiously diverse, cosmopolitan community rife with forms of Platonic body/spirit dualism. Platonism often took two forms: Stoicism ("The inner soul is the thing of value in humans. Therefore, let us discipline the body and its appetites into a rigid ethical framework. Morality is a sign of maturity.") and Epicureanism ("The inner soul is the thing of value in humans. Therefore, who cares what we do with the body? Morality is for the immature."). Paul finds himself answering questions raised by both philosophies. Paul counsels them to comprehend their lives through a new lens: redemption of the whole person—body and spirit as an inseparable whole, all of which have been ransomed by God from the "Egypt" of their former lives into the "Promised Land" of life in Christ.

Although sexual activity outside the covenant of marriage is the dominant image in this passage, one's appetite for food and the temptation to gluttony is also included. The central problem appears to be the power of the individual will to control the body. Stoic attitudes will be addressed by Paul in chapter 7; here he is dealing with the Epicurean mode of thought: "Who cares what I eat or with whom I have sex? My spirit is still intact and faithful, right?" Building on his argument in the first verses of chapter 6, Paul reveals a truth about their baptismal identity: "But you were washed clean, you were made holy to God, and you were made right with God in the name of the Lord Jesus Christ and in the Spirit of our God" (6:11). Their baptism was not a bid for self-improvement and the presence of the Spirit in their lives isn't contingent on their good moral behavior! Rather their bodies, minds, and spirits all have been wholly transferred—buried and raised—into a new life.

This season after Epiphany guides us to ask, what is God revealing about Godself and about humanity, and what response is most appropriate given this recognition? God raised Jesus, body and spirit, and God will also raise us. God has paid a price for you, not to transfer you as a slave from one despotic master to another, but to redeem you from slavery altogether. Yes, you are free women and men, Paul says. Still, he pushes past this point and asks repeatedly, "Don't you know . . . ?" Don't you know that God is as concerned with your body as with your spirit? Don't you know that relationship with Christ is similar to marriage? That your spirit is intertwined with his? That your body and the acts it performs have deeply spiritual implications?

When he states, "You have been bought and paid for," Paul is using the language of slave redemption, paying the purchase price of a servant to set them free. However, it seems that God doesn't see this price so much as a ransom as a dowry! Slaves are set free from external control and are thereby permitted to exercise bodily autonomy in the social sphere. They are set free from the fear of punishment in the exercise of that autonomy. Spouses, however, are set free to love, honor, cherish, and respect their partner while they pursue their autonomy. The Corinthians have been redeemed from the former for life in the latter. Paul says what we would say to any couple preparing to marry: in marriage, "you don't belong to yourselves." If the cross is God's dowry payment, then the raising of Jesus is the proposal and our baptism is the wedding itself. God "put a ring" on us. And, in this relationship, we are assured of finding deeper levels of satisfaction for every appetite than we dreamed possible.

Bringing the Text to Life

No text rubs against the Western grain more thoroughly than this: "Don't you know that you have the Holy Spirit from God, and you don't belong to yourselves? You have been bought and paid for, so honor God with your body" (1 Corinthians 6:9). Particularly here in the United States, we often think of ourselves as a nation of rugged individuals and bootstrap-pullers. To those who would question our autonomy or use of liberty, we offer, "Don't tread on me." On this Sunday, one might choose to focus on the relationship between the individual believer, the community of faith, and the Triune God, all three persons who figure importantly in this text. Likewise, I would invite you to elevate the importance of church membership in our development as disciples.

-7

For a couple of decades now, church leaders have denigrated the concept of membership in the church as nearly irrelevant to the life of faith in Christ. Many pastors have led their members, councils, and boards through books with titles like *From Membership to Discipleship*, casting "mere" membership in the church as an inadequate token of faith, as if formally uniting with a congregation has almost nothing to do with following Jesus. In all honesty, this can indeed be the case, just as a wedding can potentially have little to do with marriage when one or both spouses bear little intention to keep their part of the covenant. Don't get me wrong, discipleship is crucial and contains within it the vitality necessary for a long-term commitment to God and neighbor. Nevertheless, formalizing that commitment through ritual among the gathered faithful is a beautiful, essential part of the journey. Whether at the time of our baptism or later in life's journeys, we need ways to acknowledge, publicly and formally, that we do not belong to ourselves. We belong to Christ and his church.

I have found this particularly difficult in our COVID-19 and post–COVID-19 culture. At the church I serve, we have lost some families because they didn't like the decisions that our COVID-19 team made during the pandemic. Some people were upset that we ever closed in-person worship a single day! Others couldn't believe we would ever take the risk of returning to in-person worship. Some have gone elsewhere to participate in churches with policies they like better. Others disagreed with the choices of the team, but understood themselves as part of a "family" that remains faithful to one another in spite of some disagreements. As I write, some UMCs are holding town halls and votes on disaffiliation from The UMC. How much disagreement can we bear before we elect to "divorce" our church and seek another partner-congregation? Just how seriously should we take Paul's admonition "you don't belong to yourselves"?

Consider asking some of your church members, old and young, to reflect on the nature of church membership as a sort of marriage, that moment when we decided to stop "sleeping around" and "put a ring on it." Ask them how deciding to partner with a specific faith community at a specific place and time has impacted their lives. And be sure to ask them about the times of conflict and disagreement they have experienced in church. How did they get through these times and remain committed to God and neighbor over time? Perhaps you could record short videos of their reflections or invite them to offer a brief witness during worship. This might be a good Sunday to review the vows of membership in your tradition in order to ask, "How does the 'outward and visible sign' of our membership vows curb our 'wandering eye' enough to keep us faithful to the 'inward and spiritual grace' of long-term commitment to a faithful-but-imperfect community? The United Methodist vows ask us to concretize our abstract notions of discipleship: prayer, presence, gifts, service, and witness. Might church membership lead to a deeper sense of discipleship with *these people in this place*? Are we willing to let ourselves belong to God in concrete ways *through* our "marriage" to one local church?

January 21, 2024–Third Sunday after the Epiphany

Jonah 3:1-5, 10; Psalm 62:5-12; 1 Corinthians 7:29-31; **Mark 1:14-20**

Sam Parkes

Preacher to Preacher Prayer

Beloved, you saunter into my Galilee today and amble down to the lakeshore where I fish for meaning. My nets, always in need of mending, feel so inadequate as I lower them beneath the vast mystery of these texts. Help me recall that moment when I first heard you speak my name while fishing other seas. Or that moment when I swallowed your very good news—hook, line, and sinker. Teach me yet again how to fish in these water-words, confident that your Word longs to be caught. Amen.

Commentary

These verses relate three brief, timeless scenes that compose a segue between the arrest of John and a Sabbath service in a Capernaum synagogue. By "timeless" I mean that Mark doesn't indicate how much chronological time elapses over these scenes between Jesus's announcement of God's reign and the calls of the disciples. This text is more concerned with the *timing* (*kairos*—1:15) of these events.

There are clear allusions in both vocabulary (via the Septuagint) and form to the call of Abram in Genesis 12. In both stories, God initiates a relationship with a family, commands a response, makes promises to the called, and elicits a prompt, positive reaction. The promise made to Abram will be carried through his "beloved son" Isaac (compare Mark 1:11 and Genesis 22:2 in the LXX) and Jacob/Israel's twelve children and their multitudinous offspring. Similarly, Mark describes God's creation of a new "Israel" at God's initiative through Jesus the Beloved Son into whom all of the authority of Yahweh is poured. This new Israel will be generated by God's creative word spoken into the workaday lives of the Twelve. The positive and immediate responses of Simon, Andrew, James, and John (as well as Levi in 2:14) mirror those of Abram and Sarai and build toward the naming of the twelve apostles in 3:13.

In this Epiphany season, what is Mark revealing about Jesus? First, Jesus is not a "mere" rabbi or scribe like others of his day; rather, he is endowed with divine authority to create this new family, a point made even more clear in 1:21-28. Second, Jesus doesn't act like your run-of-the-mill first-century rabbi! Such teachers offered their teachings and waited for students to come to them to persuade the rabbi to take them on as disciples. Instead, the Markan Jesus is a teacher who commands, promises, and calls with all the authority of God. He emerges from the Jordan to stride with energy and confidence into the intersection of two worlds: the cosmic world of a heaven torn open, God, angels, Satan, and demonic forces and the earthly world of wilderness, rivers, lakes, prisons, and fisherfolk and their families. At this point in the Gospel he handles both with ease. In him, God's divine reign is pushing into, impinging upon the human plane of activity with authority, intention, and purpose. All of this raises a key homiletical question that simply must be dealt with in preaching this passage.

Is the response of these fishermen intended to be a model for our discipleship? Their keen response to Jesus's command is daunting. Were Jesus to stride into our own places of business with such pointing and pushing, I doubt many of us or our hearers would close the cash drawer, hang up our aprons, and leave Mom and Dad to fend for themselves in the family biz. Careful preachers will remind their listeners of Jesus's first parable in chapter 4. The story of the four soils reveals that one type of soil is *petrōdēs* or rocky: "When people hear the word, they immediately receive it joyfully. Because they have no roots, they last for only a little while. When they experience distress or abuse because of the word, they immediately fall away" (4:16-17). Just before this story, Jesus renames Simon by calling him Peter—*Rocky!* Jesus will call him by yet another name in 8:33: Satan. The Brothers Zebedee will also order up positions of power but please hold the mess of servitude and suffering, OK? (10:35). These men are not quite paragons of gospel virtue. They, like us, will fail him, deny him, betray, and desert him.

Nevertheless, into our domiciles and workplaces Jesus still strides, pushing God's way into all our little ways, commanding us to follow him, to watch him, to listen to him. The Rabbi will demand that we place our relationship with him above all else including career, family, possessions, and privilege—all the things we hold most dear. "Change your hearts and lives, and trust this good news," he beckons, "and I'll show you how to fish for people." Ah, there's the kicker! Jesus promises to give our lives new purpose, one that doesn't violate our authenticity but somehow enhances and fulfills what is most true about us. One could do worse than organize the sermon around that idea.

Bringing the Text to Life

This passage functions in two ways that can inform how preachers might approach the sermon: revelation and response. Picking one or the other will help unify the sermon around a single thrust.

First, who is Mark revealing Jesus to be? The pacing of this initial chapter is breathless and peripatetic. As a character, Jesus is forceful, clear about his mission, and initiative driven. Scenes change rapidly without copious details to hamper the pace.

Think about times that the reign of God got pushy, elbowing itself into our sense of time, timing, and space, urgently demanding a response:

- A family struggling with housing appears at the church needing assistance for a place to stay the night as well as access to helping agencies and programs in your community.

- A Black Lives Matter protest and rally has been quickly called by area churches and clergy in response to a shooting. You and your congregation are asked to participate.

- Your spouse and family have grown tired of the ways you so easily sacrifice time on your days off for work-related tasks. They have surprised you with an intervention of sorts, asking you to outline a plan with them to protect your sabbath and family time.

Rather than focusing on our response, one might spend the time discovering other contemporary situations that might be recognized as cognates to Jesus's bursting into our little fishing concerns. To admit that these moments are infused with divine energy is to admit that God is not merely present in our lives, but active and working with pushy, even obnoxious, vigor into our wallets, calendars, homes, and offices. Let the sermon deal with this fact: we want to believe in a God who is at work in our daily lives, but would often prefer that God not interject so surprisingly into our awareness and plans.

Second, what responses might these moments of inconvenient grace elicit from us? In each of the above situations, one is going to make a response. We might choose to ignore, subvert, or immediately invest in ourselves in God's reign, but we will choose. Each of these certainly could reveal Christ's kingdom call for immediate response. How does one analyze them? If you agree that, yes, this is indeed Jesus's Spirit all up in your business, what interior or exterior obstacles might we recognize in ourselves and how do we pray for God to quickly remove them from our complacent hearts to make faithful following possible? The call to follow Jesus is surely divine grace that *expects* to be greeted by our willing spirits. But such announcements can also cause a lot of trouble and prompt our resistance.

January 28, 2024–Fourth Sunday after the Epiphany

Deuteronomy 18:15-20; Psalm 111; **1 Corinthians 8:1-13***;*
Mark 1:21-28

Laurie Moeller

Preacher to Preacher Prayer

God of mercy and grace, during this season of Epiphany, enable us to hear your voice above all other voices, especially our own. Grant us an open mind and a deep thirst for your simple truth. Amen.

Commentary

All four texts for today speak to the influence and power authority has on our faith. In Deuteronomy 18, we are asked to distinguish the voice of prophets called by God, discerning the authority with which they speak. The first chapter of Mark reveals the authority with which Jesus speaks and ultimately overcomes evil spirits. Even Psalm 111, an acrostic poem, teaches the power and authority of God in creation. However, the passage from 1 Corinthians seems to shed light on a pressing issue in the life of the church both in the first century and today—who has the corner market on Christian authority and what responsibilities accompany such authority?

Corinth, a thriving city known for its wealth and the intellectual pursuits of its citizens, would have been a challenging place for faith in Christ to bloom. The discrepancies in social classes among believers would have been more obvious than in some other churches of the time. The community would have a diverse makeup of people with regard to education and social status. Many of the people with whom Paul worked were poor; however, the people of wealth (with influence and authority) were also part of the Corinthian church. Unlike many of our churches today, this was a church with people with all kinds of social standing worshiping together.

While we all long to see a church with members of diverse social standing, such diversity ultimately unveils a very relevant tension within the church regarding authority. Inevitably, those with more education and more exposure to history, theology, and philosophy often pull rank on those who do not. Paul is speaking to a group of people in the church who have the authority of knowledge but are using it to divide and unnecessarily interfere with new Christians as they seek to remain faithful and loyal to Jesus. Paul is clearly angered by the interference and uses the issue to teach about humility and the responsibility we have to one another above and beyond our knowledge.

The eating of meat sacrificed to idols is not in and of itself egregious. However, for those who have recently been a part of idol worship and have turned away from that practice in exchange for a life with Jesus, the eating of such meat would, in fact, feel wrong and unsettling. For those who know better, those who have both experience and knowledge enough to understand that idols are nothing but a figment of imagination, the eating of the meat is no big deal. But Paul is telling these experienced and knowledgeable Christians that if it is a big deal to someone else, then it is a big deal to the whole community. If it is a stumbling block for someone, then let it go and don't eat the meat!

Knowledge can lead to arrogance and arrogance can lead to a real problem in a faith community. As pastors, we should certainly see how knowledge lends authority and yet with authority comes responsibility. When we claim to have a deeper spiritual knowledge, we in turn dismantle our spiritual authority with arrogance. Paul tells those professing spiritual authority in Corinth to check their knowledge with love, lest their knowledge destroys another's faith. Knowledge puffs up and ultimately blows up a person's faith! Love builds up and ultimately raises others up in faith. Paul reminds them of the Shema, which shall continue to be a guiding light for all who seek to lead or to serve with authority: Love the Lord your God with all your heart and with all your soul and with all your mind and with all your strength and love your neighbor as yourself (Deuteronomy 6:5; Matthew 22:39; Mark 12:31-33; Luke 10:27).

Bringing the Text to Life

Paul's words to the church in Corinth speak into a present-day rift among Christians who have differing opinions on authority in the church. We would all do well to remember that knowledge puffs up and prevents us from approaching with humility and love those who see the world from a different perspective. The call for all of us to move past what we know and embrace being fully known by God, and therefore fully loved and embraced by God, will enable all of us to walk through difficult waters within the church. While we who have had a great many years of Disciple Bible Studies, extensive exposure to books and podcasts on the latest exegetical teachings, and either a long tenure in the pew or pulpit, or both, believe we know how to do church best , Paul would ask that we check ourselves with love.

Longevity in the church does not give us an individual freedom to ignore the health and welfare of the overall community of faith. Longevity does, however, lend itself to a greater responsibility for others' needs over and above our own. What we may believe about any number of social issues and who has the authority to say who is "right" may not translate to new Christians, still getting their spiritual feet underneath them. We must walk alongside one another in love and mutual respect. Freedom in Christ does not give us freedom to look down on our brothers and sisters because they don't "get it" like we do. When we are grounded in love, when we put away our puffed-up persona and meet people where they are, we might find that we have a lot to learn from those who have less "knowledge" than we do. We might find that Jesus is waiting for us to put down our commentaries and join him on the outside where people are just trying to make it through the day. Paul's words to the Corinthians challenge us to put more effort in being known by God, embracing the embrace of Jesus that surpasses all other authority. If what we know about God prevents us from loving others, we might not know much about God at all.

February 4, 2024–Fifth Sunday after the Epiphany

Isaiah 40:21-31; *Psalm 147:1-11, 20c; 1 Corinthians 9:16-23; Mark 1:29-39*

Laurie Moeller

Preacher to Preacher Prayer

God of all creation, refresh our memories and remind us again of your abiding presence. May we never forget who we are and, more important, who you are. Amen.

Commentary

The words of Isaiah for today are appropriate for the season of Epiphany as they speak to the continued manifestation of God's glory in the world. Isaiah 40 is considered to be the first chapter in "second" Isaiah, as the prophet's words shift from addressing an Assyrian-dominated Jerusalem to a Jerusalem now dominated by Babylon. The people of God are exhausted, waiting for God's deliverance, and losing hope that God is going to rescue them. As parents and grandparents cling to an old, historic promise that is fading with the passing years, what are their children learning about God's strength and power? Other gods look more and more impressive with each passing year. Other powers are more relevant and exciting to their present circumstances than this God of Abraham and Jacob who is noticeably absent from their present reality.

Isaiah 40 sits in the context of Babylon's victory. The people of God have not been faithful to God's instructions and they are truly exhausted from the continued beating from Assyria and now Babylon. They have lost their trust in God and cannot see any hope in their historic faith. These are dark days and the stories of Abraham and Moses are wearing thin considering the seeming favor shown to other world powers. They have been in exile; they have been forced from their homes; they have seen the holy temple destroyed; they have "sat along Babylon's streams crying because there they remembered Zion" (Psalm 137:1 ESV). No wonder they are faint. No wonder even the young are tired. And no wonder they are interested in considering these shiny new gods of Babylon! The suffering of God's people feels endless and the recollection of the promised land is fading into the depths of their memories. Isaiah speaks into this suffering with a loud and sure voice—God is still God. Don't you know? Have you not heard? Isaiah is asking the people of God to remember their history, remember their covenant, remember the enormity of their God. Even when the depths overshadow and the darkness is intolerable, Jerusalem is asked to remember God's presence, as the psalmist notes: "If I came to the very end—I'd still be with you" (Psalm 139:18b ESV).

Bringing Text to Life

The words of Isaiah are timeless and necessary for all generations. Every generation grows weary and exhausted by the tragedy and suffering of the earth. Every generation encounters events beyond human imagining that cause us to question God's power and presence and forget God's promise. Wars, pandemics, poverty, natural disasters, suicide, racial injustice—in addition to personal individual grief and sorrow—plague every age. We all need to respond to the invitation to look up at the sky and consider: Who created these? We all must be reminded to remember who created it all and the magnificent power and love with which we were all breathed into being. We all need to be prompted by the questions "Don't you know?" and "Haven't you heard?" because life can certainly cause us to forget.

Our faith is built upon the faith of others who have come before us; therefore, generations to come will rely upon our faith stories and our willingness to hope in the Lord only to discover that our strength was in fact renewed. Our congregations, like Jerusalem, are tired and distracted by all kinds of shiny gods that appear more powerful and more effective. Our congregations are filled with people who have worked hard, served on committees, given faithfully, and continue to see suffering and injustice and internal dissension. They see their friends pass away and their faith grows weak in the face of denominational conflict. In the face of hardship, they are enticed by the siren call of our culture to hoard resources, turn inward, and neglect the needs of their neighbors. The job of the preacher is to get them outside to see the stars and the moon and consider the vast horizon that only hints at the vastness of God's glory. We must invite them to look up and remember how God has been faithful to God's people in the past.

Isaiah speaks into the difference between human limitation and Holy strength. Our vulnerability and our weakness allow God's strength to shine and our faith to grow. The real threat to our lives and our hope is not all the tragedy on the earth or the frailty of our bodies. The real threat is our lack of memory of the everlasting God whose understanding is beyond human reach, giving power to the tired and reviving the exhausted. How are we ensuring that the generations to follow will know the stories of God's strength? During the suffering and the trauma that will continue to challenge us we must keep telling our children about Jesus and the continued promises of God. We must continue to share the stories of God raising God's people up on eagle's wings, bearing them on the breath of dawn, making them shine like the sun. In Babylonian Exile as in modern-day darkness, the people of God will always have a story of God's strength. We will always have memories of overcoming. Today is a good day to share those stories, to share our own personal epiphanies of the everlasting God and a good day to invite others to join us. Someone needs to hear our story and we need to tell it!

February 11, 2024– Transfiguration Sunday

2 Kings 2:1-12; Psalm 50:1-6; 2 Corinthians 4:3-6; **Mark 9:2-9**

Laurie Moeller

Preacher to Preacher Prayer

Holy God of wonder and mystery, as we move from Epiphany to Lent, grant us eyes to see your power and presence in the world around us and in the thoughts within us. Give us courage to speak of your truth even when we do not fully understand. Amen.

Commentary

While Mark is known for keeping things moving at a steady, quick pace, he does not hasten the story of the Transfiguration. His version only differs slightly from Matthew and Luke, telling us that the details of the experience were extremely important. The experience of the Transfiguration needed to be reported carefully and intentionally.

Mark places the Transfiguration in the center of his Gospel—right between the baptism of Jesus in chapter 1 and the resurrection of Jesus in chapter 16. The preceding stories include the Pharisees *looking* for a sign, the healing of a man who could not *see*, and Peter's inability to *see* the suffering of Jesus as a very real part of God's plan. Following the story, the disciples *see* a large crowd and the large crowd catches *sight* of Jesus. The story of the Transfiguration is a story about seeing the embodiment of the Holy in Jesus, and Peter, James, and John are granted a glimpse of the fulfillment of God's divine plan in that moment.

The story includes vivid images and symbols that all work together to reveal a truth that could not be explained or presented with just words. They all must travel up the high mountain, they must be above everyday life and experience, where the wind is whipping, and the air is crisp, and the views expansive. When they arrive, they are alone. Jesus transforms in appearance—amazingly bright and alarmingly white. Only after he is transformed are they joined by two others, and right away Peter, James, and John recognize them as Elijah and Moses. The two figures are the spiritual embodiment of the Prophets and the Law and in this moment, they are comingling with the living embodiment of the new covenant.

Peter has a flash of an idea to capture this holy trio in a shrine or tent of some sort. God is not interested in Peter's idea and quickly squashes it with a cloud and a booming voice declaring that in fact Jesus is God's beloved son and they are to listen to him. In just a few verses, the stage is set for a theophany—a visit, a sighting, an experience of God's splendor and wholly otherness—a moment that cannot be captured because it defies time and place. This is a moment reminiscent of Moses on Mount Sinai in Exodus 34 with his brightly shining face and the cloud cover of God. It is a moment referencing Elijah's meeting with God on Mount Horeb in 1 Kings 19. It is a moment in which Peter, James, and John were given eyes to see what their minds could not possibly grasp.

Bringing the Text to Life

Transfiguration Sunday pivots the congregation from Epiphany to Lent. While Epiphany is the season of the appearing and manifestation of the divine plan for the world in Jesus Christ, Lent is the season that makes that appearing and manifestation personal and relevant to our own personal stories of faith.

Peter, James, and John walk down the mountain, pivoting to a new reality having seen a vision they could neither share with others nor explain to themselves. They are set apart from the others, having now seen the healing of Jairus's daughter (Mark 5:37), the Transfiguration, and soon they will be the only guests at the garden of Gethsemane (Mark 14:33). They are the ones who will eventually put all the pieces together and start inviting people to join them in the New Covenant. Somehow the story of transfiguration is a point of no return—they have seen too much.

If Mark were writing a stage production, the intermission would take place right after Peter, James, and John walked off that mountain, still muttering some confusion about Elijah as the stage goes dark and the curtain comes down. The audience would mentally prepare for the next phase of the story. The mystery of that moment must hang in the air for a little bit before we are ready to go deeper into the journey to which God calls us. The season of Lent is a season for brave souls who have been on the mountain, seen the miraculous healing powers of Jesus, and yet know that our relationship with Jesus is more than a spectator sport. We have more to do, more to see, and more to become in our story of faith.

I wonder if the message of Mark's story of the Transfiguration is an invitation to stay for the second act—to continue into deeper waters and encounter even greater miracles than what we saw in act 1. I wonder if this is the day we recognize that holy work is scary and inexplicable and does not always translate to others. I wonder if this is the Sunday when we choose to see that which can only be seen through the Spirit—through a deep encounter with God that goes beyond where we have already been. This might be the day when we choose to engage in a mystery that will lead us to the garden of Gethsemane and ultimately to the foot of the cross so that we might see the wonder of the Resurrection.

February 14, 2024– Ash Wednesday

Joel 2:1-2, 12-17 or Isaiah 58:1-12; Psalm 51:1-17; 2 Corinthians 5:20b–6:10; **Matthew 6:1-6, 16-21**

Chris Jones

Preacher to Preacher Prayer

God, forgive me for performing for human audiences rather than directing my attention to you. Thank you for the discomfort of Ash Wednesday, and for the restorative grace your coming makes possible. Help me to live as your disciple. In the name of Jesus Christ, I pray. Amen.

Commentary

Few words catch our attention more than "Be careful." I imagine many of us remember our parents using these words when we left the house. *Be careful when you ride your bike to school. Be careful when you cross the street. Be careful when you're out with your friends.* Jesus uses these words out of concern for our spiritual well-being: "Be careful that you don't practice your religion in front of people to draw their attention" (Matthew 6:1). Then, like the master preacher/teacher he was, Jesus gives accompanying examples to this admonition: giving money to the poor (vv. 2-4), prayer (vv. 5-6), and fasting (vv. 16-18).

It's strange, though, isn't it? We read Jesus's command here about not publicly practicing our faith. But then on Ash Wednesday we seem to do just that! After engaging in corporate prayer, during the service, we come forward for the imposition of the ashes. We stand before the pastor (or whoever is administering the ashes) and receive the sign of the cross on our forehead, a visible, tangible sign of our religious faith. How are we are not contradicting what Jesus says?

To be clear, Jesus's concern in this passage is *not* with religious practices. Indeed, the practices he mentions—generosity, prayer, and fasting—are worthwhile acts, designed to bring us closer to God. Moreover, Jesus assumes we are going to engage in these practices (He doesn't say, for example, "If you pray" but "When you pray.").

Rather, Jesus's concern is that when we engage in these acts, we have the correct audience in mind. The problem with the hypocrites (presumably the Pharisees and legal experts whom Jesus identifies as hypocrites in Matthew 23) is they perform for a human audience rather than directing their attention to God. In each of the examples he cites, Jesus says the hypocrites engage in these acts purely out of a desire for human recognition (vv. 2, 5, and 16).

Of course, Jesus's use of the word *hypocrite* is also telling. Nowadays we think of a hypocrite as a person who says one thing and does another. However, in Jesus's day the word *hypocrite* had a different meaning. Hypocrites were actors who spent their days entertaining audiences. As such, Jesus's use of *hypocrite* is apropos: those who engage in religious acts for human attention are not focused on God; they are performing for others. Jesus's concern is not with the act but with the heart. Therefore, we don't have to fear the public nature of the ashes so long as our hearts are in the right place.

There is an additional reason we are not contradicting Jesus's words. The hypocrites whom Jesus has in mind think of themselves in superior terms. However, the ashes are a concrete reminder not of our superiority but of our humility. Indeed, few acts are more humbling than having somebody tell us we are dust and to dust we shall return. The ground is level at the altar. We all stand in need of the redemptive grace of God. The ashes aren't a sacrament, but in a sense, they are sacramental: they are an outward and visible sign of a spiritual reality. The reality is that we are broken and it is only through God that we receive salvation.

Bringing the Text to Life

1. John Wesley once referred to All Saints' Day as "a festival I truly love."[1] It may sound strange, but I've always felt the same way about Ash Wednesday. I love the honesty of Ash Wednesday. While our culture conditions us to avoid unpleasant topics like sin and death, Ash Wednesday shows up on the liturgical calendar (of all days this year, on Valentine's Day!) and confronts us with the truth—we are mortal; we don't have it all together; we are weak and helpless, in desperate need of God to save us. Perhaps T. S. Eliot puts it best: "Why should [human beings] love the Church? Why should they love her laws? She tells them of Life and Death, and of all they would forget. . . . She tells them of Evil and Sin, and other unpleasant facts."[2] Praise God for the "unpleasant facts" of Ash Wednesday!

2. I have always been intrigued by the term "imposition of the ashes." After all, when do we ever use the word imposition positively? We throw out sentences like "I'd like to stay for dinner, but I don't want to impose." What are we saying, then, when we call this ritual the imposition of the ashes? We are saying that we are doing something that (quite frankly) makes us uncomfortable. We are acknowledging our brokenness and frailty and that it is only through Jesus that we receive forgiveness and eternal life.

3. When I was in high school, I was asked to deliver a talk on spiritual growth. Not being very confident in my preaching skills, I took advantage of a practice session hosted by my church. Around the table were various adult leaders prepared to

give feedback. After I nervously delivered my talk, one of the adults picked up the Bible I brought and, looking at all the pages that were underlined and highlighted, said, "Chris, you really read this Bible!" The problem was that the Bible didn't belong to me, but rather, my mother. Yet for some reason that man's words made me feel important, so I didn't correct him. I learned that day the desire for human attention runs deep in me. It even led me to lie about reading the Bible after delivering a talk on spiritual growth! Thanks be to God for forgiveness and grace (and that I'm not too embarrassed to share this story).

February 18, 2024—First Sunday in Lent

Genesis 9:8-17; *Psalm 25:1-10; 1 Peter 3:18-22; Mark 1:9-15*

Chris Jones

Preacher to Preacher Prayer

God, thank you for remembering us. Even though we human beings are prone to forgetting, you never forget us and you never stop working for our good. I love you and praise you for your mercy to us. In the name of Jesus, I pray. Amen.

Commentary

The story of Noah may be the most familiar in the Bible. But even in the familiar God speaks to us in new ways. As I was studying this passage, the words "I will remember" (vv. 15, 17) kept rising to the surface.

After following God's lead in the construction of the ark and enduring the turbulence of the floodwaters, Noah and his family are given permission to leave. However, God's work isn't quite finished. Shortly after Noah and his family depart, God issues the same commandment that he originally gave to Adam and Eve: "As for you, be fertile and multiply. Populate the earth and multiply in it" (Genesis 9:7). How can those departing from the ark populate the earth (as Adam and Eve and their descendants did) while knowing that another flood may come? After all, while the flood was cleansing, it did not completely rid the world of sin. Human beings will continue to mess up and get it wrong.

God alleviates the concern for another possible flood through the covenant God initiates. This covenant isn't simply meant for human beings but for all of creation (Genesis 9:9-10). Moreover, God declares that the visible sign of this covenant, the rainbow, will help God remember the promise he makes not to flood the whole earth. The covenant, like so much of scripture, demonstrates God's commitment to remembering.

Prior to chapter 9, the text tells us God remembered Noah and his family, as well as the animals onboard, when the floodwaters ceased and the waters began to recede (Genesis 8:1). God also shows this same kind of remembering when sparing Abraham from the destruction that overtakes the cities of the valley (Genesis 19:24). Sometime later in Genesis God remembers Rachel and her desire to have a baby (30:22). Finally, in the book of Exodus, God remembers the Israelites when they are enslaved in Egypt (Exodus 2:24). In truth, God's remembering isn't limited to the Old Testament. The New Testament contains examples of divine remembering. For instance, in the book of Acts, God remembers Cornelius's gifts to the poor and sends the Apostle Peter to proclaim the gospel message to this non-Jewish man.

It's worth noting that in all these instances, whenever God remembers, God *acts* on behalf of the ones he's remembering. God's remembering, therefore, is more than an intellectual activity. It's more than a recalling of people, places, or events. Rather, it's a precursor to divine action. Through remembering, God unleashes God's power in the world. God "shows up" through acts of mercy and grace. Let's be honest. We human beings tend to be distracted, scattered, and forgetful. However, we serve God who constantly remembers.

The above message is a welcomed one, especially given the challenging situations we sometimes face. The preacher would do well to remind his or her congregation of the good news that God has not forgotten them. Rather, God remembers them in their plight—whatever the plight may involve—and, in some mysterious way, is working for their good (Romans 8:28). It's not that God causes hardship (hardships are a product of life, not of God), but God actively works to redeem hard circumstances. The God of the rainbow, the God of the covenant, the One who remembered Noah and his family and the entire world following the Flood, remembers us, too. Moreover, through that remembering, God demonstrates powerful acts of good.

Bringing the Text to Life

How long do famous people stay in the public memory? The answer is between five and thirty years. This information is derived from Cesar A. Hidalgo, director of the Collective Learning group at the MIT Media Lab.

In January 2019, Hidalgo and colleagues sought to determine how long people and products remain in the cultural picture. As preachingtoday.com (where I derived this illustration) puts it, "They traced the fade-out of songs, movies, sports stars, patents, and scientific publications. They drew on data from sources such as Billboard, Spotify, IMDB, Wikipedia, the US Patent and Trademark Office, and the American Physical Society."[3] After doing this research, the team designed mathematical models to calculate the rate of decline. They found that "the universal decay of collective memory and attention concludes that people and things are kept alive through 'oral communication' from about five to 30 years."[4]

While human beings, individually and collectively, tend to be on the forgetful side, the story of Noah and other parts of scripture powerfully remind us that God doesn't forget. Instead, God holds fast to the promises he makes.

The Lion King (1994) is my all-time favorite Disney movie. When I think about the relationship between God's remembering and divine action, I'm reminded of the scene where Simba (the younger lion) is distraught and discouraged over the death of his father. Suddenly, he looks up in the night sky and sees the image of his late dad, who calls out from the clouds with these words, "Remember who you are." After remembering his own identity, Simba immediately goes to reclaim his rightful place as king of the Pride Lands. Simba moves from memory to action. This shift illustrates the wonderful truth we find in the Bible that whenever God *remembers*, God *acts*.

February 25, 2024–Second Sunday in Lent

*Genesis 17:1-7, 15-16; Psalm 22:23-31; Romans 4:13-25; **Mark 8:31-38** or Mark 9:2-9*

Chris Jones

Preacher to Preacher Prayer

God, thank you that in Jesus you did not resist the cross. You refused to allow others to stand in the way of your intended mission. Thank you for sacrificially giving yourself to us. By grace, help me to follow in your example as I sacrificially give myself to you and the good news of your kingdom. In the name of Jesus, I pray. Amen.

Commentary

I don't remember everything I learned in school (do any of us?). However, while reading Mark 8:31-38, I couldn't help remembering something my undergraduate New Testament professor once pointed out. On three separate occasions in the Gospel of Mark, the reader encounters a threefold pattern: (1) Jesus predicts his suffering and death, (2) the disciples misunderstand what Jesus is saying, and (3) Jesus uses this misunderstanding as an opportunity to teach about discipleship. In addition to Mark 8:31-38, we find this pattern in 9:30-37 and 10:32-45. This pattern supports Mark's overall Christology: Jesus as suffering messiah. Put simply, Mark wants the reader to understand that the cross was not a divine afterthought; rather, the cross was the culmination of Jesus's ministry. That's where all this was headed. If the Crucifixion was Jesus's coronation, the cross was his throne.

Mark begins his Gospel by announcing "the good news about Jesus Christ, God's Son" (1:1). However, he then seems to conceal all references to Jesus's messianic identity and sonship. For example, shortly after the Gospel begins, Jesus silences an unclean spirit who declares Jesus to be "the holy one from God" (1:23-25). And even the disciples are told to keep quiet following Peter's bold declaration that Jesus is the Christ: "Peter answered, 'You are the Christ.' Jesus ordered them not to tell anyone about him" (8:29b-30). Why all the secrecy?

To be clear, it's not that Mark doesn't want the reader to know Jesus's true identity as the Messiah and the Son of God; rather, the Gospel writer wants the reader to *understand* the entailments of this identity. For example, if Peter had properly understood what it meant for Jesus to be the Christ, he wouldn't have reprimanded Jesus for speaking about his suffering (8:32). Clearly Peter had something besides the cross in mind. Perhaps Peter expected Jesus to be a political ruler who would liberate Israel from Roman occupation. Suffering redeemer wasn't on his list! It's worth recognizing that Peter was correct in his declaration about Jesus; however, the expectations behind that declaration were incorrect. Of course, it's easy for us to criticize Peter. But how many of us come to Jesus with the wrong expectations? How many of us are guilty of trying to make Jesus fit into our categories?

It isn't until the crucifixion when Jesus takes his last breath that the picture comes into focus. Mark writes, "When the centurion, who stood facing Jesus, saw *how he died*, he said, 'This man was certainly God's Son'" (15:39, emphasis mine). The Gospel ends the same way it begins, with a reference to Jesus as God's Son. However, there is no longer a need to conceal Jesus's identity because the centurion (irony of ironies that the centurion grasps this point before the disciples do) properly connects it with Jesus's death.

We serve a suffering messiah whose glory was displayed at the cross. Further, our messiah invites us to actively give ourselves to him and the good news his coming inaugurates as he has given himself to us. Jesus's invitation to discipleship isn't directed exclusively to the disciples. Mark notes he called "the crowd together *with* his disciples" (8:34, emphasis mine). Jesus intends for all of us to hear these words and to take up our cross and follow him. The road will never be easy, but we answer this call within the bounds of divine grace, trusting that God will empower us every step of our journey.

Bringing the Text to Life

Some things are hard to unsee. Think of certain store logos. Baskin-Robbins cleverly displays the number 31 in its logo, reminding us that the store serves thirty-one flavors of ice cream. FedEx strategically places an arrow in between the *E* and the *x* of its logo, telling us that FedEx is on the way to deliver our package. The logo for Tostitos shows two people enjoying a chip over a bowl of salsa. It's hard to unsee these hidden messages once we notice them. Similarly, it's hard to unsee the threefold pattern of Mark 8:31-38 or Jesus's concealment of his messiahship/sonship throughout the Gospel. However, once we notice these features, we can help our congregation explore why they are there.

Peter's expectations involving the Christ were wrong. How many of us have had our expectations challenged? In August 2005, a woman entered a radio contest after hearing the DJ promise the tenth caller a prize of 100 grand. Imagine the woman's shock and disappointment when, after winning the contest, she didn't receive a check, but instead, a Nestle's 100 Grand candy bar. She ended up filing a lawsuit with the station.[5]

N. T. Wright tells the story of an archbishop who was approached by three teenage boys. The teenagers asked if they could confess their sins. However, the archbishop sensed their insincerity; they were trying to make a joke of the whole matter. Eventually, two of the boys ran away laughing, but the archbishop managed to say to the third young man, "Okay, you have confessed these sins. I want you to do a penance. I want you to walk up to the far end of the church and I want you to look at the picture of Jesus hanging on the cross, and I want you to look at his face and say, 'You did all that for me and I don't care that much.' And I want you to do that three times." The young man broke down in tears, unable to complete the task. As Wright notes, there is something about Jesus's sacrifice that moves even the most hardened among us to love-filled repentance.[6] Our Lord did not resist the cross.

March 3, 2024–Third Sunday in Lent

Exodus 20:1-17; Psalm 19; **1 Corinthians 1:18-25***; John 2:13-22*

Jasmine Rose Smothers

Preacher to Preacher Prayer

Only Wise God, as we reach this third week in the Lenten season, intentionally drawing near to you is becoming more difficult. Please do not allow us to lose sight of the journey to the cross. Give us a fresh anointing to "blow the trumpet in Zion" (Joel 2:1 NIV) and encourage your people to observe a Holy Lent. Allow us to surrender our strength and wisdom for the foolishness of the powerful cross, O Lord, we pray. Amen.

Commentary

Who determines the difference between "foolish" and "wise"? Is wisdom dependent on context or perspective? Is foolishness defined by experience or reason? In 1 Corinthians 1:18-25, the Apostle Paul draws distinct lines between those who understand the message of Christ as foolishness and those who understand the message of the cross as transformational power; between those who are "being destroyed" and those who are "being saved" (1:18); and between those who are wise and those who believe in the message of the cross.

The Corinthian church is a community located in the center of acquired wisdom. The Corinthians are concerned with status. They are preoccupied with knowledge, power, money, and even "fake news." Some are destroying the church with their "wisdom" that doubts (a) Christ crucified, (b) Christ resurrected, and (c) that the Crucifixion and Resurrection produce saving power. Thus, Paul is forced to take the believers back to the facts. Many believe Paul's "Christ crucified" message to be scandalous, foolish, and even heretical. How could such a humiliating experience like crucifixion lead to a salvific experience like resurrection? It just doesn't make sense! The Corinthians are such an educated people that their knowledge is getting in the way of their hearts.

In a day when the cross appears everywhere—on chains around the necks of many, on bumpers and windows of cars, and on doors and windows of businesses and households—it is hard to remember that the cross was a sign of humiliation. It was the opposite of the power of God (1:18). In fact, if we resist the temptation to skip from Palm Sunday to Easter Sunday and, instead, settle down into the dark of Good Friday, we might better understand that the cross could be interpreted as a sign of the failure of God to act on behalf of the Son of God. Historically, crucifixion was a very public and scandalous method of capital punishment reserved for the worst offenders. Crucifixion was meant to embarrass, humiliate, and make a statement about the power of the empire. To say that there is redemptive power through the shame of the crucifixion of Jesus can be interpreted as foolishness for those, such as the Corinthians, who seek logic, knowledge, and wisdom as status symbols.

Yet, Paul reminds the Corinthians of a promise from Isaiah: "I will destroy the wisdom of the wise, and I will reject the intelligence of the intelligent" (1:19). In other words, those who hang their hats on how much they know will be left with nothing. God has leveled the playing field. The experts will be left with no status. You can't have enough degrees to be closer to God. Paul continues: "Where are the wise? . . . Hasn't God made the wisdom of the world foolish?" (1:20). Human wisdom means nothing, considering God's wisdom. The only thing that will sustain us in this world is the power of the cross.

This text is an equitable reminder for all of us during the Lenten season. There is no pecking order in God's economy. Everyone must seek the Lord for themselves. The believers must experience the power of God through fasting, sacrifice, confession, and repentance. Drawing near to God through believing that God *is* leads to a transformational encounter with the crucified Christ. Access to the power of God does not come from status, education, money, or power. You can't work your way, earn your way, learn your way, or pay your way to the cross. You can only believe your way to the cross. And yes, through human eyes, this may feel ridiculous and foolish. It is countercultural and antithetical to society's way of life. Yet, in God, it is wisdom (1:21).

Bringing the Text to Life

Plans for the Easter Egg hunt are starting to distract from our promises to God on Ash Wednesday. Work and family commitments are so numerous that we're starting to forget and crave those things we gave up or took on for Lent. The scandals of the twenty-four-hour news cycle are louder than the scandal of the cross. We must be reminded of why we observe a Holy Lent and why our commitments to our spiritual journey matter.

The text says: "Instead, God was pleased to save those who believe through the foolishness of preaching" (1:21b). Is our preaching "foolishness" to those who don't believe? Or are we preaching what is acceptable to our cultural norms and the people with status in our virtual and in-person communities? How will they know to look beyond signs and wisdom for Christ crucified? How will they know that what we've turned into ordinary is extraordinary? How will they know that they are called to

"God's power and God's wisdom" over the world's status (1:24)? How will they know unless we preach the foolishness of the cross? What foolishness is happening in your community? Preach a fearless sermon that juxtaposes the latest scandal in your community with the scandal of the cross in the time of the Corinthians.

The Epistle reading ends like this: "This is because the foolishness of God is wiser than human wisdom, and the weakness of God is stronger than human strength" (1:25). As we invite people to struggle with their humanity, their scandals, and their relationship with Christ during this Lenten season, let's also empower them with the folly that God's wisdom may seem foolish to us, but it is power to those of us who need a Savior!

March 10, 2024—Fourth Sunday in Lent

Numbers 21:4-9; Psalm 107:1-3; 17-22; **Ephesians 2:1-10**; John 3:14-21

Jasmine Rose Smothers

Preacher to Preacher Prayer

Loving God, as we worship this fourth Sunday in Lent, draw us close to you. Remind us of your grace and mercy. Reveal your goodness through every generation that we encounter this week. Enable us to see life where others have declared death. Remind us that your salvation is a gift. We cannot earn it. We cannot possess it. You gave it to us, and you sustain us in it. We thank you, O God. In the mighty name of the crucified Christ, we pray. Amen.

Commentary

Ephesians 2:1-10 is instructive to the church and community during the Lenten season. The season of Lent is a season of reflection, intentionality, acknowledgment, and confession of our sin and repentance—in the true sense of the word—to turn away from and not return to the behavior we have given up. Ephesians 2:1-10 is an invitation and encouragement to observe a holy Lent:

- The text provides the reason we need the Lenten season: "At one time you were like a dead person because of the things you did wrong and your offenses against God" (2:1). We need this time to realize and acknowledge our sin in the world. In the Wesleyan tradition, we much prefer to talk about grace over sin. However, during the Lenten season, we must instruct our congregations to take inventory of our wrongs. If we do not, we will continue to live lives that are not pleasing to God and, worse, lives that are dead.

- The text summarizes the intent of the Lenten season: "However, God is rich in mercy. He brought us to life with Christ while we were dead as a result of those things we did wrong" (2:4-5). The Lenten

– 31

season allows us to experience the abundant life that Jesus promises. Through the mercy of God, we do not have to remain dead. We are entitled to abundant life if we accept God's mercy to move us beyond our wrongs and into life with Christ.

- The text explains the activity of the Lenten season: "He did this because of the great love that he has for us. You are saved by God's grace!" (2:5). The Lenten season ushers God's people into an awareness of God's love and grace for us and unto us. It's easy to miss this if we rush through the Lenten season. It's important to highlight that we cannot work our way into God's love. In a society focused on what one has earned, pointing to the countercultural nature of God's love, salvific power, and grace is critical.

- The text reminds us of God's purpose and intention for the Lenten season, not just for us but for all: "God did this to show future generations the greatness of his grace by the goodness that God has shown us in Christ Jesus" (2:7). God saved us by grace, not because of us, not because of anything we did, but because God loves us and because future generations need to know the goodness of God. Often, we get so focused on ourselves that we do not count the cost of our behavior for those behind us. The use of the resources (people, financial, economic, emotional, mental, climate, water, food, time, relational, etc.) that God gives us has generational implications. Are we passing on God's goodness in how we use God's resources now? Will future generations know that God is good through our behavior right now? Will future generations experience God's grace through our faith? Will they have a scarcity mentality or a generosity mindset based on how we react to the goodness of God in our lives?

- The text points to our responsibility in our individual relationships with God and the result of the church's commitment to the Lenten season in the lives of the community: "You are saved by God's grace because of your faith. This salvation is God's gift. It's not something you possessed. It's not something you did that you can be proud of. Instead, we are God's accomplishment, created in Christ Jesus to do good things. God planned for these good things to be the way that we live our lives" (2:8-10). We are saved by grace because of our faith. The entire action is God's because you live your faith. This understanding presupposes that faith is a critical element in salvation. Hebrews 11:1 reminds us, "Faith is the reality of what we hope for, the proof of what we don't see." The Lenten season is a journey of faith. It is, as D. T. Niles reminds us, "one beggar telling another beggar where he found bread." It is both individual and communal. "We're all just walking each other home."[1] Faith is an intentional growth process. We receive the gift of salvation through faith because God created Jesus and us to do good things. May this Lenten season be a "good thing" that forms how "we live our lives."

Bringing the Text to Life

One of the old hymns of the church says,

> Very deeply stained within, sinking to rise no more;
> But the Master of the sea heard my despairing cry,
> From the waters lifted me, now safe am I.
> Love lifted me! Love lifted me!
> When nothing else could help, love lifted me.[2]

The remaining verses are just as impactful. Preaching through this hymn might be a powerful way to engage the congregation. It may help them name their sin and recognize God's presence to transform us all.

Think back to verse 7. Using testimony as a part of the sermon (either live or via prerecorded video) could be a powerful way to demonstrate God's goodness now and for future generations. Illustrating God's grace and goodness in tangible ways can be transformational for all the gathered people.

March 17, 2024–Fifth Sunday in Lent

Jeremiah 31:31-34; *Psalm 51:1-12 or Psalm 119:9-16;*
Hebrews 5:5-10; John 12:20-33

Jasmine Rose Smothers

Preacher to Preacher Prayer

Gracious God, speak to our hearts. Holy Spirit, sustain us, renew us, and empower us. As we encounter this fifth Sunday in Lent, grant us your joy and remind us that you are with us. Help us to stay focused on the journey to the cross—even as we prepare for loud hosannas and Easter celebrations. Thank you for the assurance of being your people, dear Lord. In Jesus's name, we pray. Amen.

Commentary

Covenant is a gift from God. God initiates it. God sets the terms. God invites us into God's covenant. All of the instigating activity is on the side of the Almighty God. God always keeps up God's part of the covenant. People fail or break covenant with God. Jeremiah, the reluctant weeping child prophet turned reluctant complaining adult prophet, gives humanity hope beyond destruction and hope for a new covenant. In Jeremiah 31:31, the text reads, "The time is coming, declares the LORD, when I will make a new covenant with the people of Israel and Judah." While we're clear that God's time and our time are not the same things, we now have the benefit of expecting a future with hope.

The new covenant "won't be like the covenant I made with their ancestors when I took them by the hand to lead them out of the land of Egypt. They broke that covenant with me even though I was their husband, declares the LORD" (31:32). This new covenant is good news. Everything has been destroyed. Israel as a nation, the tribes of Israel, their homes, their families, the temple, the people's promises to God—everything has been destroyed. After all of this, Israel is scattered in exile and it's hard for them to know where they stand with God. Yet, they misunderstand that

God's nature is good, loving, redeeming, and restoring. They have forgotten that God is with them in the midst of it all.

This covenant will be different. The Israelites will not need tablets or rabbis to read the covenantal instructions for them. God says, "I will put my Instructions within them and engrave them on their hearts. I will be their God, and they will be my people" (31:33). Do you know what it's like to have people? In popular vernacular, to have a person or to have people is to have someone you can always count on, someone who will come through for you, someone who is on your side and is at work for your good. Your "person" knows you inside out. To have people means that someone no longer operates out of obligation in a relationship, but they have made a conscious choice to do good to you and for you and to, by choice, live in the mutuality of the relationship. We know the nature of God, but the nature of people has proven flaky in Jeremiah. The Lord is now saying that God will have "people." God's people will not follow the covenant by obligation and compulsion. Instead, God's people desire to be in covenant with God and choose to follow the instructions that they now know for themselves and in their hearts. The Hebrew Bible translates the word *husband* in (31:32) as "master"—as one who legislates, compels, forces, or requires obedience. Through this new covenant, God now comes alongside those who choose and desire to be obedient to their God.

This new covenant signals a turning point in the Lenten season. As we mature and take on this identity as God's people, we should move from "I gave up Coke for Lent, and I can't wait to get one on Easter Sunday" to "I offered up a sacrifice/behavioral change/habit to God (I turned away from it—repentance) and I'm so glad that I'll never go back to it." We move from obligation to transformation; and from being held hostage to freedom. The scripture continues, "They will no longer need to teach each other to say, 'Know the LORD!' because they will all know me, from the least of them to the greatest, declares the LORD; for I will forgive their wrongdoing and never again remember their sins." A shift. A choice. A love. An intimacy. A desire. A transformation. The covenant is no longer about compliance; the new covenant is about collaboration. The new covenant is for everyone ("from the least to the greatest"). The old covenant kept score and counted wrongs. The new covenant forgives and frees.

I've heard it said that the church is the only institution that exists for those who are not yet a part of it. This ideology builds on the old adage that "the church is a hospital for sinners, not a hotel for saints." The Lenten season is the perfect time to act on these visions of the church. As we move toward the end of Lent, Jeremiah 31:31-34 provides an opportunity to help our congregations see our commonality in God. We all need the new promised covenant. We all need God's instructions engraved in our hearts rather than stuck in our minds. We all need to know the Lord for ourselves. We all need our sins forgiven and forgotten. Whether we've observed and executed a perfect Lent or we've never heard of the Lenten season, we are all in need of this transformational covenant and this transcendent God.

Bringing the Text to Life

This week's pericope provides an excellent opportunity for a children's sermon on the differences between promises, contracts, and covenants. Highlight that it is God who starts, crafts the terms of, and sustains a covenant. Point out the difference between human activity and God's action in the work of covenants. The children's moment would be an opportune time for the entire congregation to interact in the worship service—in person or online.

This text lends itself to vivid storytelling. Be sure to include the historical, biblical, and theological context so that the understanding of the covenant can be as robust as possible.

March 24, 2024–Liturgy of the Palms/Passion, Sixth Sunday in Lent

Psalm 118:1-2, 19-29; **Mark 11:1-11**

Will Willimon

Preacher to Preacher Prayer

Jesus, we have been walking with you on your journey toward Jerusalem. Now, as you come into the Holy City and things look dangerous, we are not so sure that we want to walk all the way with you. Lord, stir us to boldly step up and join your parade, even if that parade is moving toward a costly cross. Open our eyes to see you as our last, best hope; our way to abundant life; our parade toward your peculiar glory. Amen.

Commentary

On Palm Sunday Jesus parades into Jerusalem as well as into our lives. His is a curious parade. We expected him to come in triumph and with power, he comes in among us in weakness and in humility. We wanted him to take charge and free us from all that ails us; he suffers and dies for us. On Palm Sunday we come together as a church and we are confronted with a core question: Will we join up, join in, and take our places in Jesus's parade?

Palm/Passion Sunday is the entrance into the holiest time of the Christian year, the Sunday when we joyfully parade into Jerusalem so that we might be able to fully parade out of the empty tomb next Sunday.

Jesus's identity is misunderstood by the adoring crowds. Jesus is forced to keep explaining to his own disciples what he is talking about in his parables (Mark 4:10-13, 34). Finally, Peter confesses Jesus as the Christ (at the same time appearing to misunderstand the significance of his peculiar discipleship) only to be rebuked by Jesus and called Satan after he rejects Jesus's self-understanding as one who must suffer and die (Mark 8:27-33).

We continue to be shocked that the very Son of God must suffer rejection, suffering, and death on the cross.

This Sunday we take our places in the most curious of parades, a procession that seems to change direction midway through, turning from our false messianic expectations toward the true Messiah who wins his victories through suffering and death.

Our job as preachers on Palm/Passion Sunday is to recruit people with the guts to walk in this parade that leads to the cross.

Bringing the Text to Life

One of my most vivid memories of childhood was the Greenville Christmas Parade, circa 1954. I had the unimaginable good fortune of being pulled out of school early to watch the parade. There were platoons of Shriners, and floats from the PTA, the FFA, 4-H, and every notable organization in town. The climax of the parade, of course, was Santa Claus, seated on an impressive float, in a sleigh pulled by a John Deere tractor.

This tradition, of every kid in town marching behind Santa Claus, was just about the only time I can remember from my childhood when all the kids in Greenville, white and Black, came together. Greenville was legally racially segregated. Black and white were divided by laws that made our one town into two towns. We were racially separated, segregated except for this one time in the year. All of us joined together and marched behind Santa and all of us drank the same hot chocolate, something we were legally prohibited from doing any other time of the year.

I didn't know it at the time, but that Santa Claus parade, in which I joined with all the other kids in town, regardless of race, was like a walk into the future. It was a parade into the world that was coming even to Greenville, a world in which the two races lived and worked as one.

I remember when I finally summoned the courage, as a student, to walk in a parade protesting racial segregation in South Carolina. I went to that civil rights demonstration with a couple of friends. When I got to the area where the demonstration was forming, I was stunned that there were hundreds of people in attendance. I wasn't alone in my convictions. People from all over who wanted to be part of this parade, a parade not of celebration but of protest. In the march, we began singing with one voice, "We Shall Overcome." Marching as one, singing as one, we became one. I came away from that parade stronger.

Today, Palm/Passion Sunday is a favorite day for parades in the church as we process with palm branches and sing "Hosanna!"

Jesus, whose ministry has mostly been limited to the hinterland, now at last arrives in the capital city, the Holy City of Jerusalem. Presumably, there were lots of folks present who were getting their first glimpse of Jesus.

A throng of excited well-wishers welcome Jesus by waving palm branches. Some take off their coats and spread them along the route—a traditional sign of honor and welcome.

The Roman overlords who occupied Judea at this time may have gotten nervous when they heard the shouts and saw the reaction of the people of the city. Periodically, the Romans would assemble their troops in Jerusalem and march through the city streets just to show Jerusalem who was in charge.

When Hitler's troops took over Paris, they marched in triumph through Paris's Arc de Triomphe just to show the Parisians who was boss.

In sharp contrast, just behind the waving branches and the shouts comes an unarmed man, bouncing on the back of a donkey. He was not riding a strong, impressive war horse like any general; he was on a donkey. This was the long-awaited messiah?

This parade was a jolt to popular expectations for lordship, for salvation, and for liberation. Still is.

My questions: Will you come forward and join this parade? Will you walk behind Jesus as he moves down his narrow path this coming week, as we move from shouts of "Hosanna!" to a mob screaming, "Crucify him!"? Will you lay aside your preconceptions of salvation, deliverance, and power and take your place in this parade?

Welcome to Holy Week. Come, let's join Jesus's parade wherever he takes us this week. Come, join the parade.

March 28, 2024–Maundy Thursday

Exodus 12:1-4, (5-10), 11-14; Psalm 116:1-2, 12-19;
1 Corinthians 11:23-26; **John 13:1-17, 31b-35**

Will Willimon

Preacher to Preacher Prayer

As we accept Jesus's invitation to come to his table and partake of his body and blood on this holy day, may each of us receive a new sense of Christ's presence among us. Thank the Lord, Christ comes to us in the daily stuff of life, in bread and wine, in his gathered body, the church, and in ordinary words spoken by an ordinary fellow Christian, the sermon. God with us, thanks be to God. Amen.

Commentary

Tonight, Maundy Thursday, we partake of the Lord's Supper, a sacrament. John gives us an account of Jesus's final meal with his disciples just before he goes to suffer and die in their behalf. We commemorate that last meal that John so eloquently describes, but we also do more than recollect and remember. We are not simply reenacting his last supper. We vividly experience Christ's presence with us. Tonight, here at the table, God gets down on our level.

We are animals, not flighty, spiritual beings. We are creatures who live here, in the shadow of Calvary, land of blood and torn flesh, in bondage to booze. All around us people are perishing from too little bread, and more of us are perishing from too much bread and wine, a socially acceptable narcotic. While many are in bondage to excess, little children cry through the night for just one piece of bread and, and . . . that's where Jesus meets us.

Because we could not, knew not how, had not the means to come to God, God came to us. We can't climb up to God through our good works, our projects, our noble ideals, our beautiful services of worship. So God climbed down to us. Tomorrow, between noon and 3:00 p.m., we're going to see just how far God will go to save us.

Bringing the Text to Life

We will give you a piece of bread and a sip of wine and promise you that God is here. What's going on here?

Saint Augustine could say in a sermon before coming to the Lord's Table that it is not as if this bread is made holy because it's in a church and the bread you had at home for breakfast this morning is unholy. Rather all bread is a holy gift of God, a sign of God's presence, but we, numbed and dumb as we are, can't see it. That is, can't see it until the priest lifts up the loaf and exclaims "holy," then the sacrament becomes a window to see what's going on among us.

The great challenge being worked out tonight, at the table, is not how we can make God present among us, for God always is, but rather how God gets to us, we who are forever rummaging about elsewhere, so distracted and preoccupied by ourselves that we can't even see the bodily presence of Christ among us.

What's going on tonight is that God is getting to us. Jesus makes a promise to us, "The bread is my body given for you." The bread becomes, in this act, a tangible, specific gift for you. For you. That's what I, in my bumbling attempts to preach, try to tell you. Having tried to tell you, tonight we show you.

It really is amazing what lengths God will go to get to you.

As the Reformer John Calvin said, God never forgets, in dealing with us, that we are creatures, not angels. Therefore God deals with us in ways that creatures can understand: water, bread, and wine.

Tonight, for you, God gets specific, as specific as broken body pieces of torn bread, as explicit as blood-red wine. I'm sorry for those of you who think that Christianity is ethereal, "spiritual." It's as corporeal, carnal, and concrete as what you had for breakfast this morning. God likes matter; God invented it.

What a gift this is for those of you for whom faith is difficult, for whom belief does not come easily. This bread and wine are given for you.

All God asks is your empty, outstretched hands to receive a gift. Tonight, this is all about what God does, not what you do. Grace. Gift. Listen to his promise at the table: "This is my body given for you."

Thank God that God does not wait around for our understanding of all this, or our faith to firm, in order to come to us. While we are so earnestly trying to believe and to think our way to God and "get it," Jesus says simply, "Here, have some bread, my body; wine, my blood, all of me, body and blood, for you."

In Jesus's story of the Prodigal Son, he says that when the son turned back home from the "far country," his father did not wait for him to get all the way home. Rather, the father ran out to meet the boy, to embrace him, to fix him a feast.

If God waited until we got to God, we would never. So God gets to us. My body and blood, for you.

When he says, "For you," he implies that anything less bloody, less costly, deep, dark, and mysterious, whatever it would be, it wouldn't be for you.

This night, in Jesus, God the Father has come all the way down to our level, has come all the way out to meet us.

This body, this blood, given for you.

March 29, 2024–Good Friday

Isaiah 52:13-53:12; Psalm 22; Hebrews 10:16-25; **John 18:1-19:42**

Will Willimon

Preacher to Preacher Prayer

On this highest, holiest, most somber and sacred day of the church's year, what is there to be said? Jesus, Son of God, Savior of the World, is tortured to death, all somehow part of our salvation. We preachers cannot hope to add to the wonder of this mystery, to explain its significance or plumb the depths of its meaning. Lord, help us simply to tell the story well and then to point to its deep significance. That will be enough to make this bleak Friday good. Amen.

Commentary

The story that John tells so vividly in his account of the trial and crucifixion of Jesus is a dramatic account of a God so determined to be Emmanuel, God-with-Us, that he goes even unto death.

Who is God? Nine out of ten will say that God is large, up there, out there, aloof. God the judge who sets high a moral bar we will never chin up to. God the Creator who messed up by creating us and now puts as much distance as possible between us disappointing creatures and God's high and mighty divinity.

John's Gospel and Good Friday say otherwise. Though from the first we turned away from God every chance we got—our pride, lust, idolatry, injustice, and smart-mouthed sin are well documented—God turned toward us, suffered, died, paid, and now reigns. God in action.

"Christ died for our sins," "Jesus paid it all," "We've been saved," "Brought from death to life," "He bore our curse." This a truth so deep that it takes a dizzying array of metaphors to talk about it—and still there is much left unsaid.

"I'd do anything for my family," parents often say. When God said it, God meant it; God did it. Any God who is determined to reconnect, reconcile and redeem people like us must not be squeamish about shedding blood, for we have a long history of murdering our saviors. Love hurts. God loves us to death.

After his cross and resurrection, Jesus's people raced throughout the world with the good news that "God raised crucified Jesus from the dead!" Naturally, somebody asked, "Who has been raised from the dead? What did he say? What did he do?" The next question was, "What's the meaning of what has happened in Christ?" Thus, Christian theology was born. God was in Christ, in his crucifixion, doing much the same atoning work as in the creation of the world, or in liberating Israel out of enslavement.

Somehow, someway God turned the cross, an instrument of shame and suffering, into a sign of God's victory over our sin and death, God dealing decisively with our self-distancing from God. That's the wonder that gathers the church on Good Friday.

Next time you find yourself wondering "Just who is God and what is God up to?" Next time you ask the question behind all our God questions, "Is God loving and is God's love there for us?" remember what you see and hear on Good Friday.

"Lord, how much do you love us?" we asked. "This much," Jesus answered. And he stretched out his arms on the cross and died.

Bringing the Text to Life

The story that John's Gospel wants to tell us this night can be hard to hear. Crucifixion is one of the most vicious, publicly humiliating forms of capital punishment ever devised. Excruciating. Look what we have done to God's son.

Jesus didn't die peacefully in his sleep; he was agonizingly tortured to death, receiving nonviolently the world's violence. Crucifixion is Roman public murder that's disturbingly analogous to American lynching.

"He came unto his own, and his own received him not" (John 1:11 KJV). He offered us open-handed fellowship. Our collective response? Well, you heard it, "Crucify him!"

The cross is a mirror that reflects who we really are as well as a window where we are given a privileged look into the heart of who God is. Who are we? Those who on this Friday afternoon viciously rejected God. Who is God? The One who raised crucified, despised, betrayed Jesus from the dead, the One who decisively, graciously rejected our violent refusal.

A crucified Messiah? The thought that God's Anointed would suffer and die as a common criminal was unthinkable. God Almighty, willing to be pushed out of the world on a cross, deserted by his closest friends, held up for the world's scorn and ridicule.

If there was any way John could have cut out this story or sugarcoated it, he would have. We know the story of the cross is true because this is the way humanity has always responded to a loving God. Look what we've done to God's Son.

Yet when we've done our worst—put to death God's only Son—God turns our sin into the means of our salvation. Look what God has done with our sin. Remember that, next time you either do or receive the worst.

March 31, 2024–Easter Day

Isaiah 25:6-9; Psalm 118:1-2, 14-24; 1 Corinthians 15:1-11;
John 20:1-18

Will Willimon

Preacher to Preacher Prayer

Lord Jesus, on this grand day you defeated sin and death and rose to new life. In this time of worship, come to us, minister to our fears and doubts and raise us to new life. May we, in this hour, not only sing about your resurrection victory but come to believe in your triumph. May we not only adore you in our worship but follow you forth into the world as we show forth in our lives and in our words, "We have seen the Lord! He is risen!" Amen.

Commentary

Last Sunday, Palm Sunday, we focused on the journey that characterized Jesus's entry into Jerusalem. John's account of the resurrection appearances is characterized by a number of "journeys" to and from the tomb: Mary Magdalene arrives at the tomb and next there comes Simon Peter and the Beloved Disciple (20:1-2). Simon Peter and the Beloved Disciple go to the tomb and then they return to their homes (20:3-10). Mary, just outside the tomb, meets the risen Christ and is commissioned by Christ to bear witness to the Resurrection. She and Christ then leave the tomb behind (20:11-18) as they go forth.

Three different people coming to the tomb and leaving the tomb in three different ways.

Mary comes to the tomb fully expecting to find entombed there the dead body of Jesus. That's not what she finds. Even then Mary does not recognize him but thinks he is a "gardener." The Beloved Disciple comes to the tomb then sees and believes. Simon Peter comes, sees, and sort of believes. Three close friends of Jesus, coming and going to the empty tomb in different ways.

Perhaps there are a number of people in the congregation who, though they hear the triumphant music, listen carefully to your sermon, and see the beauty of a church decked out for Easter, will still say, "I'm just not sure."

Can we proclaim the resurrection of Jesus Christ in a way that might help them move toward a more sure faith in the truth of Easter?

Bringing the Text to Life

Each of us comes to the mystery of the Resurrection from different perspectives. For some of us, belief in the truth of Easter is immediate and easy. For others of us, it takes time. However we come to the mystery of God's defeat of the powers of sin and death in the resurrection of Jesus, the risen Christ will find a way to make himself known to us that we might believe and then go forth to tell the world, "He is risen!"

For some of you, you hear the idea of a crucified Jew, entombed for three days, and you may say, "Sure, I've believed in the truth of resurrection since I was a child."

Others of you may see all these flowers and hear the joyful Easter music or listen to my sermon and in the end say, "I'm just not sure. I don't really believe that I believe."

Some of you may come to this joyful morning full of joy and happiness. Easter Sunday is your favorite Sunday of the church year. You have been rehearsing the music, or looking forward with great anticipation to this Sunday for a long time.

Others of you may be in gloom rather than in light. You have just lost someone whom you love. You may find all this joy and triumphant gladness to be somewhat oppressive.

It took Mary Magdalene a while to believe in the Resurrection. It was only when Christ called her name that she was able to announce to the disciples, "I've seen the Lord." It took the other disciples longer to believe what they had seen with their own eyes.

Where are you in this story of the first Easter? For some of you, it's quite enough for you to come to church, see the flowers and sing the songs, and you steadfastly, firmly believe, "He is risen!"

Others of you come to church, see the flowers, sing the songs, hear the sermon (!) but come away muttering, "I just can't say for sure. I just don't know what to believe."

Still others of you see all the evidence, hear the complete testimony, and scripture's rationale for believing but you are waiting. For you, resurrection faith is not so much intellectual assent as it is waiting for your name to be called: "Mary," or "John," or "Lea."

How have you come here this Easter morning? What path has brought you here?

It doesn't matter how you have come here. What's important is the promise implied behind today's Easter gospel: the risen Christ is not here, not entombed in a dead, ancient past. He is risen! He's on the move! Moving toward you, eager for you to see and, in seeing, to believe, wanting to give you what you need in order to believe, calling your very own name.

In his resurrection, who did Christ appear to? His own disciples. To some, the risen Christ called their names. To others, he simply stood before them. He seems determined to connect, intent on giving them whatever they need to believe that his love and life are triumphant, and not only a triumph for him, but for them as well.

I don't care how you come to Easter. Christ's promise is that you won't go away the same. You, even amid your questions, doubts, or reservations—Christ will give you the faith to be able to say to the world, in one way or another, "I have seen the Lord!"

April 7, 2024—Second Sunday of Easter

*Acts 4:32-35; Psalm 133; 1 John 1:1-2:2; **John 20:19-31***

Alex Shanks

Preacher to Preacher Prayer

O God of the Resurrection, come to us now, even as we sit behind closed doors, huddled in fear, filled with doubt. Stand among us and speak to us Your word of peace. Breathe on us Your Holy Spirit so that we might fully believe and be sent forth to bear witness to Your love in this broken world. In the name of the risen Christ we pray. Amen.

Commentary

The passage begins with the disciples huddled in fear behind closed doors. Here comes Jesus to stand among them and offer peace. Jesus confronts the fear and disbelief of the disciples with straightforward, clear action. He shows them his hands and side and breathes on them the Holy Spirit. Their collective response is joy.

Thomas is the outlier. He missed the big reveal. He couldn't accept the words of the others. He wanted to see for himself. Can we blame Thomas for insisting on some proof? Wouldn't we likely do the same?

We tend to look down on the doubt of Thomas, even unnecessarily branding him with the nickname "Doubting Thomas." What if doubt is not a problem but an opportunity? What if doubt is always a prelude to faith? What if wonder and curiosity are prerequisites for growth? Notice that Jesus does not sidestep or condemn Thomas's doubt and questions. Jesus invites Thomas to place his finger here and his hand into his side. Through this gracious invitation to come and see for himself, Thomas gets a full glimpse of who Jesus is and professes a renewed faith in Christ, whom he now realizes is both Lord and God.

Thomas stands as a pivotal figure in the Christian story. While many of the disciples got to see, touch, and hear Jesus, we *don't* have that opportunity. A new stage of church life and faith begins with this story of Thomas. Thomas's declaration is clear and compelling: my Lord and my God. What if all of us could profess the same?

Did you notice that Thomas missed seeing Jesus in the first place because he had left the room where all the disciples gathered? The story doesn't say why but, you know, everybody deals with death and loss in different ways, and my guess is he was just one of those people who needed to work it out on his own, all by himself. There is nothing wrong with that of course but we really need to stay together. We will find what we really need for belief most clearly in community. Thomas's downfall may not have been his doubt but rather his trying to do it on his own.

A preacher once told the story of a ninety-seven-year-old woman who, looking back, said she had learned the most important lesson of her life when only a child. She and a group of friends had decided one afternoon to climb Mount Washington in New Hampshire. Before they were able to descend, a late afternoon fog rolled in and enveloped them all in its thick, obscuring whiteness. They couldn't see the way ahead, so they agreed they would move down the mountain very slowly, inch by inch. And they agreed they would all hold hands and would not, under any circumstances, let go of one another. Remembering the event years later, the woman said of this experience: "Sometimes . . . all I knew or could see of the world was the hand ahead of me and the one behind. Sometimes my arms ached so badly I thought I would cry out loud, but that is how we made it at last. We found our way home by holding on to one another."[1]

What a metaphor for the significance of maintaining community, relationships of trust with other searching and faithful people. Of course, we'll still undergo the challenges of those girls on the mountainside. Sometimes we'll get lost. Sometimes we'll be strained to stay together, strained by our differences, though we share a faith. Sometimes we'll be unwilling or unable to trust what the others are telling us or to credit their insights into the way ahead. But if we can hang together, we can cover some pretty rough terrain, safely and securely.

Bringing the Text to Life

In this culture, we say "seeing is believing," but Jesus uses this critically important moment to say "believing is seeing." Now that's a paraphrase. His actual words are "blessed are those who have not seen and yet have believed" (John 20:29 NIV). But clearly what that means is believing is seeing.

Jesus is calling us to step away from a fear-based trust in our own quantifiable ability—and toward absolute trust in the God who is in charge of death itself; the God who will accomplish things completely beyond our imagining. We should be wonderfully comforted by the fact that Jesus is willing to show us his scars if that's what's required for us to believe. But we should be powerfully attracted to the realization that God blesses belief in the absence of evidence with the ability to see in a way we could have never seen on our own.

Sometimes we need to act as if we believe something. You can act your way into a new way of feeling easier than you can feel your way into a new way of acting. You can believe your way into seeing things differently, allowing the eternity of God to break into your life.

The challenge, then, is to come together and trust God and live in light of God's love, even when we cannot always see it or feel it. Maybe in remembrance of doubting Thomas, we ought to widen our standards of proof, and invite God to envelope us with love.

All I have seen teaches me to trust God for all I have not yet seen. Let's not get ourselves mixed up in any other, smaller conclusion. Let's not settle for anchoring our minds and our beliefs anywhere else than in the total assurance of God's eternal, unending love for us!

April 14, 2024–Third Sunday of Easter

Acts 3:12-19; **Psalm 4***; 1 John 3:1-7; Luke 24:36b-48*

Alex Shanks

Preacher to Preacher Prayer

O God of righteousness, come and listen to our cries. Bind up our brokenness as we seek to fully experience the light of your face. Fill our hearts with your resurrection joy as we put our trust and hope in you alone. Amen.

Commentary

Our only hope in the shadow of the resurrection story is to create daily rhythms that remind us that God is not dead. God is surely alive. Psalm 4 is one of the traditional psalms read during compline, the final service of the day. Compline is often said in a monastery or in a personal time of prayer. It is a concluding prayer for the day and a reminder that each day should begin and end in prayer.

Whenever we recite this psalm, we can be transported once again to the reality that living as the people of God, in light of the resurrection of Christ, is only possible when we declare total dependence on our God of righteousness. The disciples in the Luke text are found terrified and afraid. They, like us, are not living in the strength and light of the Resurrection. Psalm 4 provides a path forward.

The psalmist begins with a plea: "Answer me when I cry out! . . . Set me free from my troubles!" (v. 1). Which one of us can't relate to our need for God to answer us and listen to our prayer? We wonder out loud, can anyone hear me? Is anyone listening?

The psalmist then names the core of the problem—people insulting reputations, loving worthless things, and chasing after lies. Our social media culture certainly displays these things. We inhabit a world where lies are justified by many, worthless things are cherished, and reputations are destroyed. In the midst of it all, the psalmist turns to God trusting in God's personal care of the faithful, believing that God does indeed hear our prayers.

The psalmist commits to not be afraid but instead to ponder during the night what it means to trust in the Lord. The psalmist is undeterred even when goodness is not found, or the light of God's face has left. The psalmist remembers that we have a God who fills our heart with greater joy than any material thing can bring. Peace at the end of the day comes as we fall asleep fully aware of this God whose presence alone is our safety and our hope.

It has been only a few weeks since we celebrated the Resurrection. The joy of that moment is short-lived. The psalmist returns us to the reality of everyday life, a life where there are insults, a life void of the light of God's face. We need to turn back to God.

Psalm 4 provides a blueprint for a life of prayer. We too can learn to cry out to God and ask God to answer us. We can trust that God's mercy is real even when we pray, "How long?" We can have knowledge and trust in the Lord who takes personal care of us. We can fall asleep at once and in peace, knowing that God is with us to give us safety and strength. Nothing can compare to a life lived in response to the Resurrection.

Bringing the Text to Life

The Psalms are God's invitation for us to sit down in the midst of life's circumstances and experience God's grace and love in new ways. The Psalms are so much more than a book of quotes to pull out on occasion. The book is meant to shape our lives, form our souls, teach our hearts, and transform our faith. This is a prayer book with a mission. What we see as a random grouping of words is designed to be an intentional and holistic journey of faith and hope. The Psalms are meant to change the way we live. Many would describe the Psalms as the greatest hymn book, the greatest prayer book, the greatest gathering of wisdom and theology that the world has ever known. It is a book we need more of in this very moment in life.

The world is full of chatter and noise. In fact, we are so scared of silence that we typically run from it. To make matters worse, much of the noise in the world doesn't help us live life to the fullest, instead it drowns out the very voice of God in our lives. The problem is many of us have become tone deaf.

Remember, God is after what is in our hearts. God isn't concerned about our outward appearances. And what's in our hearts is a direct corollary to the scripture we mediate on. The goal of learning and studying the Psalms is so our heart takes over when our mouth and mind and body are off-center. The scripture we meditate on in our hearts becomes the central calming and directive force in our lives.

So, what about you? What thought do you meditate on in the middle of the night? What scripture comes into your mind as you drive down the road, as you face fear, as you watch the news, as you struggle with relationships? God wants to give us all a new way of being through the practice of prayer.

What might it look like to invite people to increase their life of prayer? What if your church became a praying church during Eastertide? Psalm 4 could be the basis of this life of prayer. Its honest appraisal of life will resonate with many. The promise of Psalm 4 is that the Lord "takes personal care of the faithful." What greater resurrection joy can there be?

April 21, 2024—Fourth Sunday of Easter

Acts 4:5-12; Psalm 23; **1 John 3:16-24**; *John 10:11-18*

Robin C. Wilson

Preacher to Preacher Prayer

Loving God, you sent your son who showed us the way of sacrificial love. In the moments when the selfishness of our congregants turns us toward anger, remind us to be like Christ within the community. During this Easter season, restore our joy and our hope, as we place our whole trust in you. In the name of the one who came to show us a better way. Amen.

Commentary

Sacrificial living is a foreign concept in today's world. How often we are bombarded with messages to look out for our own best interests. Political parties capitalize on this as do advertisers encouraging us to spend our money on the things that will enhance feelings of self-worth and elevate us above others. Thus, when we encounter the words of today's scripture from 1 John, our congregations may balk at the "wokeness" of this ancient text! "Give our possessions away and lay down our lives? Surely, they don't mean me," would be an expected twenty-first-century response.

To begin a sermon on this, we must realize the conditioned state of our congregations. The world has taught them to look out for themselves, and then perhaps altruistically share if they have resources left over. How eye-opening it is to look at this early Christian community, receiving this message of how to live with the ethic of love. Indeed, they were challenged to move beyond the teachings of the Torah (to love our neighbor as themselves) to now the extreme example of laying down their lives for their brothers and sisters. The struggle to love sacrificially must have been real for at least some in that community. Perhaps the struggle is just as real for communities of faith today, as they wrestle with the mission and true purpose of church.

It is clear that love is expressed in the powerful combination of belief and obedience through sacrificial action toward others. Leading up to this lectionary passage, verse 11 especially reminds the reader that the author is speaking to the community of Christ followers about how they should treat one another within the community. The act of Jesus in laying down his life is lifted as the example of how radically the members of the community are to love one another, if they truly have belief in Christ.

Bringing the Text to Life

In preparing to preach this text, it would be informative to lift up the quote often attributed to John Wesley, which is not actually found in his writings: "There is no holiness without social holiness." Talking about how this quote is often used to link the necessity of belief/faith with social justice/good works would be an easy opening to then give congregations an actual quote found in the preface to *Hymns and Sacred Poems,* published in 1739:

> *The gospel of Christ knows of no religion but social; no holiness but social*
> *holiness. "Faith working by love" is the length and breadth and*
> *depth and height of Christian perfection. "This commandment*
> *have we from Christ, that he who loveth God love his brother*
> *also;" and that we manifest our love "by doing good unto all men, especially to them*
> *that are of the household of faith." And in truth, whosoever loveth his brethren*
> *not in word only, but as Christ loved him, cannot but be "zealous*
> *of good works." He feels in his soul a burning, restless desire, of*
> *spending and being spent for them. "My father," will he say,*
> *"worketh hitherto, and I work." And at all possible opportunities*
> *he is, like his Master, "going about doing good."*[2]

In this context, we read that social holiness is linked directly with doing good to those within the "household of faith." As many have engaged in difficult discussions about politics, denominational discernment, and other topics, it might do the congregation well to be reminded that we are to lay down our lives for one another within the community of believers. This does not of course exclude loving those outside of the community, which might deserve stating, yet sacrificial love and unselfishness toward one another because of belief in the salvific love of Christ is a powerful witness to the outside world.

April 28, 2024—Fifth Sunday of Easter

Acts 8:26-40; *Psalm 22:25-31; 1 John 4:7-21; John 15:1-8*

Robin C. Wilson

Preacher to Preacher Prayer

Come Holy Spirit and direct and move us as boldly as you did Philip so long ago. Give us the faith to obey you and may we not tire of sharing the good news this Easter season. Allow nothing to distract us from our calling. Amen.

Commentary

Every time I read this passage of scripture, I feel the frustration of the Ethiopian eunuch. A trusted and learned person with great responsibilities, he is trying to understand ancient theological writings that do not make sense to him. Much scholarly debate exists on the Ethiopian eunuch with regard to his anatomy, gender, social standing, race, and more. All is worthy of discussion and healthy to explore, and yet my focus today is with Philip, whose capacity for faithful obedience is remarkable in this pericope.

We remember that the believers in Jerusalem were to be persecuted by the authorities and were scattered throughout Judea and Samaria (Acts 8:1). Philip went to a city in Samaria faithfully preaching and healing, until an angel told Philip to take a road from Jerusalem to Gaza. "So he did" is the scriptural record of his response (v. 27). No rationalizing why another route was better, no whining that he was doing a lot of good in Samaria already, no excuses. Just obedience. The spirit told Philip to approach a carriage and stay with it, and Philip's response was to run up to the carriage. Not walk, run. The conversation that follows seems natural and organic after his obedience to the angel and to the Spirit. Philip and the Ethiopian explore the scripture, and with the eunuch's invitation, Philip proclaims the good news to him.

After the good news is shared on this desert road, they came to some water (v. 36). Since God has been so active in this passage up to now, I cannot help smiling thinking of God's timing as the topic of baptism must have just been discussed! It appears Philip, obedient as ever, did not hesitate when the eunuch asked if there was anything that would keep him from being baptized. Certainly there was much precedent that could have given Philip pause. This is a far cry from the pharisaical mores that could have been an influence on Philip's understanding of those who are welcome into the open arms of Christ. Yet again, we have no biblical notion of his hesitation in welcoming this new brother in Christ.

After this baptism, the Holy Spirit took Philip away to continue his faithful ministry preaching the good news until his arrival in Caesarea. The baptized Ethiopian eunuch went on his way rejoicing.

How remarkable that Philip was obedient and didn't miss the opportunity to be faithful, even when persecuted, isolated from other believers, or with people whom the Jewish authorities would have considered unworthy. How remarkable that the conversation flowed so naturally between the two men who were so different. How remarkable that God guided and directed Philip through this encounter, as well as into new ministry settings and with new people as the Spirit took him. What a story of obedience, inclusion, relationships, faithfulness, and more!

Bringing the Text to Life

Christ-followers were fleeing persecution, and still, Philip was able to hear and heed the call to share the good news in new places and with new people. We certainly would have understood if Philip hesitated. It is easy to contrast Philip with Jonah, Moses, and other hesitant biblical leaders. But every congregation has someone whom they would not be inclined to welcome with the good news. Just as the Ethiopian eunuch was different from Philip, there is a category or type of persons who differ from your congregation who could be ignored. I pastored a congregation that prided its history of inclusion so much that they didn't realize how unwilling they were to answer the Spirit's direction to share the good news with those with a history of intolerance!

How often have we not obeyed the spirit and missed the opportunity to witness to someone because we hesitate, either because of our own desires or discomfort? Where have we missed it? Where have we been like Philip and complied and been useful in ways we never imagined?

What is the calling of God today for your people to obey?

May 5, 2024–Sixth Sunday of Easter

*Acts 10:44-48; **Psalm 98**; 1 John 5:1-6; John 15:9-17*

Robin C. Wilson

Preacher to Preacher Prayer

Loving God, forgive me when I have not taken the time to praise you and sing you a new song. Forgive my preoccupation with my own tasks and busy-ness, wherein I forget about all you have done and are doing. As I continue leading this Easter season, may this psalm remind me of your awesomeness. Keep doing what you do, God, and I'll be better about singing your praises. In Jesus's name. Amen.

Commentary

Sing a *new* song. I laugh at this word choice by our psalmist, for surely the psalmist knows that our congregations balk when unfamiliar or new music is introduced into our worship. Nevertheless, the psalmist tells the people of God of the mighty acts of God that deserve a chorus of praise. The music lifted is not only to come from the people of God, but the whole of creation is to join in extolling the virtues and wonders of our God.

The psalmist seems to bubble over with gladness for what God has done and the people of God are instructed to get their instruments out and play together in a combined expression of praise. For surely, this God who has let his salvation be known will continue to work to bring it forth and establish justice. This psalm has much deeper meaning if you catch that God's people want justice to come, thus they have experienced some type of stress/duress, most often thought of in relationship to exile. If they were to come together and realize all that God had done for them in their collective past, surely they could gather and sing to the God who would give to them a glorious just future, no matter their current circumstances. All of creation can sing to the God who will establish justice over all the earth.

Bringing the Text to Life

Every congregation has its favorite hymns or praise songs that it loves to hear. Invite the congregation to think about Christmas: what are the Christmas hymns/songs that they would miss if not sung in church? Then ask about Easter Sunday or the Easter season: Is the *Hallelujah* chorus a must? Has a pastor/music leader ever deviated from those and faced backlash? After setting the tone with this lighthearted discussion, move them into a discussion of the meaning of music in worship. Does it elicit an emotional response or please a group of gathered church members, or does it give glory and praise to God?

Gently help them see how easy it is to make worship and singing God's praises about our human preferences and not about how best to please God, with music just being one example of this. Talk about other ways we forget to seek to give *God* praise with our life in Christian community, and instead make our community about pleasing ourselves.

May 12, 2024–Ascension of the Lord

Acts 1:1-11; Psalm 47 or Psalm 93; Ephesians 1:15-23; **Luke 24:44-53**

Charley Reeb

Preacher to Preacher Prayer

Remind us Lord that apart from you we can do nothing. Thankfully, you have not left us to our own devices. Your call is an ambitious one, but one not separated from the guidance and power of your Spirit. Forgive us when we seek to do your will apart from the strength you so graciously provide. Teach us Lord to give up control so that we may experience the joy that comes from surrendering to your power. Amen.

Commentary

The Ascension of Jesus Christ does not get enough love. It is often neglected in scripture and the oral traditions of the church. When we speak of Jesus's crucifixion, resurrection, his appearances to his disciples, and his glorification, not much attention is typically given to the Ascension as a specific event. In fact, Luke is the only Gospel to lift it up as a distinct historical moment.

It is easy to understand why the Ascension is often ignored. Jesus is leaving. It is sad to see him go after all he has accomplished. The Resurrection was quite the curtain call! But now Jesus must go to the right hand of God. No more appearances or words of wisdom. No more miraculous signs and wonders. Jesus is departing. Now what? How do we live until his return?

Before he departs, Jesus promises the disciples that they will receive power from God, and they should wait for it (v. 49). This power will provide all they need to live out the mission he has set forth and sustain them until he returns. The text says they will be "furnished with heavenly power" (v. 49). Jesus blesses the disciples and departs. The disciples then return to Jerusalem with joy, eagerly awaiting the power that was promised.

"Furnished with heavenly power." This sounds good! We could all use some "heavenly power," don't you think? Well, according to scripture, Jesus made good on that promise. At Pentecost, God's power infused the church. Those who profess Jesus as Lord should have that power. The church should have that power.

It is encouraging to think about all this power we are supposed to have, but, if we are honest, the church today doesn't seem all that powerful. It is clear that the church doesn't have the same influence it once had. Many would argue that the prominence of secular culture outside the church, along with the infighting and division inside the church, has rendered us irrelevant and powerless. Where is all this power that Jesus promised?

Some critics claim that the church lacks power today because it does not try hard enough to be relevant. "Many millennials see no need for the church or the faith it proclaims" is often the line given. Clever words like *nones,* those who don't claim a religious affiliation, are discussed by gurus at church-growth seminars and mentioned in a vast array of books on church leadership. At these seminars and in these books, marketing strategies are presented to reach these so called "nones." Many pastors and churches spend a great deal of time, money, and energy trying to make their church experience as enticing and relevant as the TikTok videos that mesmerize the masses.

Others use the old, tired line, "People don't go to church because it is filled with a bunch of hypocrites." It is argued that the disparity between the Jesus Christians profess and the behavior they often exhibit renders the church powerless.

While I would not disagree that there is some merit to these and other reasons given for the lack of power in the church, I believe the overriding reason why the church seems powerless is because it often neglects the very mission Jesus empowers us to live out—the mission we find in this week's text: "a change of heart and life for the forgiveness of sins must be preached in his name to all nations, beginning from Jerusalem. You are witnesses of these things" (vv. 47-48).

The power Jesus promised before his ascension is evident in the hearts and lives that are changed when the gospel is proclaimed. We are the conduits of the life-changing power of Jesus Christ. When the church refuses to be distracted and focuses on its mission of changing lives with the gospel, the power of Jesus is displayed, and it is powerful! We are "witnesses of these things"!

Bringing the Text to Life

The power Jesus promised is not seen in how "big" a church grows or how "popular" the trappings of the Christian faith become in a community; it is seen and experienced in the hearts and lives that are changed when the gospel is preached and the love of Christ is shared. A sermon around this theme should explain how the life-changing power of Jesus sets the church and the Christian faith apart from the world. The church becomes influential and powerful when it focuses on what makes the Christian faith different from the empty promises of culture. This approach is what will truly fascinate the very people we are trying to reach. After all, they have experienced all the world has to give and are still left wanting. "Do you have anything different to offer?" Indeed we do!

Tom had a good friend from college named Frank whom he stayed in touch with through the years. Frank became very successful and wealthy at a young age. He had three or four homes. He was a member of a half dozen prestigious golf clubs. He had all the nice cars and toys with all the bells and whistles.

One day, Tom could not get in touch with Frank. It seemed as if he had dropped off the face of the earth. He thought, "Maybe Frank and his wife are on a long trip through Europe."

Soon after his failed search for Frank, Tom took a group of adults on a mission trip and they visited an orphanage. The orphanage was run by a couple who adopted several kids and had taken in many more. They had a staff of people helping them. When Tom walked into this orphanage, he almost collapsed on the floor. There was Frank changing a diaper, wearing an old T-shirt and shorts. Frank and his wife had given up their lavish lifestyle to run an orphanage.

Later that night, after all the kids had been put to bed, Tom and Frank sat in the small living room and talked. "What happened to you?" Tom asked. "Well, you are not going to believe this," Frank replied, "but I was on a business trip and a coworker of mine kept bugging me to go on a spiritual retreat. So, finally, I went, begrudgingly. At that retreat I heard a man speak about how Jesus called him to start a ministry to orphans and something happened to me. It was like an out-of-body experience. Something grabbed my heart and wouldn't let go. Afterward, I called my wife and told her that things were about to change." Then Frank said, "I was just minding my own business and out of nowhere Jesus grabbed my heart. So, there is no going back now."

"A change of heart and life for the forgiveness of sins must be preached in his name to all nations. . . . You are witnesses of these things" (Luke 14:47-48).

May 19, 2024–Day of Pentecost

Acts 2:1-21; *Psalm 104:24-34, 35b; Romans 8:22-27;*
John 15:26-27; 16:4b-15

Charley Reeb

Preacher to Preacher Prayer

*Lord, may your Spirit blow on your church anew. We have become complacent and self-
centered. We have lost our zeal to share the good news with the least, last, and lost. Help
us, dear Lord, for we have become weak trying to serve your church without the aid of
your Spirit. Revive us, Lord! We surrender to the power of your Holy Spirit. As we put
aside our trite agendas, lead us to where you are working in the world and empower us
to preach the gospel and fulfill your mission of making disciples for the transformation of
the world. Amen.*

Commentary

It should not be lost on preachers that the event of Pentecost in Acts is essentially a story about the Holy Spirit empowering the church with the gift of proclamation. Last week we read in Luke that before Jesus's ascension he promised his
disciples "heavenly power" to preach "a change of heart and life for the forgiveness
of sins" (Luke 24:47-49). Now, in the "sequel" to Luke's Gospel, the book of Acts, we
read about this very power to proclaim infusing the church. "Flames of fire" alighted
each one of them and they "began to speak in other languages as the Spirit enabled
them to speak" (vv. 3-4). Interpretations abound about the event of Pentecost, but
one thing is clear: when the Holy Spirit showed up, the early Christian community
began to preach the "mighty works of God" (v. 11) in every language under heaven.
Preachers should be rather partial to the story of Pentecost because it reminds us that
"the Spirit is the power which enables the church to 'go public' with its good news, to
attract a crowd, and . . . to have something to say worth hearing."[1]

A friend of mine recalls sharing a meal with the late Billy Graham. He gathered
up the courage to ask the great evangelist a curious question. "Dr. Graham," he asked,

"when you preach, you evidence confidence that you are preaching the very Word of God. How do you know that it is indeed God's Word and not your own idea?" Graham replied, "Oh! It is when at least one person there no longer hears my voice, but hears the Other Voice speaking."[2] Billy Graham knew that the power of his preaching came not from his knowledge of scripture, his charisma, or even the strength of his voice, but from the Holy Spirit.

As preachers, we all have stories of working hard on a sermon, doing our best to make our message clear, only to find out from folks filing out of church that they heard a different sermon than the one we thought we preached! How many times have we toiled on a sermon we thought was so worthless that we wanted to run away and hide after worship only to hear someone say, "That sermon changed my life"? When I was a young pastor I would get frustrated when moments like these occurred, foolishly thinking I could somehow control the impact of my proclamation. However, as I have gotten older, and hopefully wiser, I realize how ridiculous I was for thinking I could control how the Holy Spirit chose to work through my sermons. And why would any of us want to anyway? Who else but the Holy Spirit can take our humble sermons and suit them to the variety of needs among our congregation on any given Sunday? Jesus encourages us in Luke 12: "The Holy Spirit will tell you at that very moment what you must say" (v. 12). This should not give us an excuse to be lazy when preparing sermons but it is liberating to know that the daunting task of preaching is not all up to us. This is the message of Pentecost.

Bringing the Text to Life

Pentecost Sunday is an appropriate time to remind your congregation not only of the Holy Spirit's role in the communication of a sermon in worship but also of how active the Holy Spirit is when any follower of Christ chooses to share the good news. You see, preaching is not reserved only for the ordained. Every person who professes Jesus as Lord is called to preach. They may not preach behind pulpits but they communicate the gospel with great power and effectiveness just the same. Their sermons are preached over backyard fences, in texts and emails, on social media, in bars, in the cereal aisle at the grocery line, and in line at the post office. If Pentecost teaches us anything it is that the Holy Spirit can and will speak through anyone. After all, Peter went from turning his back on Jesus to proclaiming the Pentecost sermon that converted three thousand people.

I have heard some great sermons over the years from all kinds of different people. Once, a colleague spoke of a man who has been active in his church for about twenty-five years. He became a strong man of faith and a real pillar of the church all because of a short sermon he heard while playing golf. My colleague asked him what led him to be a Christian and start going to church. The man said, "Oh, it happened on a golf course. I was paired with a man and his son for a round one day. I didn't know them, but they were the nicest people. I really enjoyed playing golf with them. I had already made another tee time for the next morning, which happened to be a Sunday. So, I asked my new friends, 'Would you like to play tomorrow morning? I really enjoyed playing with both of you. Why don't we do it again?' I'll never forget what that man said to me. He replied, 'Thank you, but I just think a man ought to be in church on Sunday.' That was twenty-five years ago, and that one sentence turned my life around."

Powerful sermons come in all shapes and sizes and, thanks to Pentecost, they can be preached by anyone at any time.

May 26, 2024—Trinity Sunday

Isaiah 6:1-8; Psalm 29; Romans 8:12-17; **John 3:1-17**

Lynn Bartlow

Preacher to Preacher Prayer

God, blow your Spirit among us. Blow your Spirit of love upon us as we seek your message for our community this week. While we are unworthy of your love, we open our lives to your Spirit to move us. Enable us, as we sit with your Word, to hear the good news in our very souls. Enable us, as we approach your Scriptures, to hear the message that will resonate with the gathered community this week. Enable us, as we approach the pulpit, to share your unfailing love with the gathered community. In the name of the one who creates, redeems, and sustains us, we pray. Amen.

Commentary

Nicodemus is a religious leader and teacher of the Law who knows Jesus and comes to speak to him. Later we will see Nicodemus again at the tomb when he helps Joseph of Arimathea bury Jesus according to Jewish customs (John 19:38-42). In describing this encounter, the author states that it takes place "under the cover of night." It is significant that this event took place in the evening, for John has established "night" as separation from the presence of God earlier in 9:4; 11:10; and 13:30. In the sentences directly after the passage for today, the author again condemns those who prefer darkness over light (3:19-21).

The exchange between Nicodemus and Jesus begins with affirmations from the man. He claims Jesus as rabbi and teacher from God. Notice that he uses plural language. "We know," he says, not "I know," suggesting the community that Nicodemus is a part of joins him in recognizing what Jesus has done. Nicodemus claims that they know who Jesus is because of the signs and wonders experienced through his ministry. The miraculous signs that Jesus performed proved he was a teacher from God. We know that Jesus doesn't want people to follow him based on signs and wonders (John 2:23-25).

In response, Jesus immediately gives him a riddle. In order to see or understand God's realm, you must be born again. Nicodemus responds to his statement literally, and Jesus continues with a spiritual answer. Jesus uses symbolic and spiritual language, while Nicodemus can't see beyond the literal meanings of the words. After last week's explosion of language, perhaps this needs greater conversation. When are we speaking different language from those we seek to address?

Jesus turned that which Nicodemus thought he knew upside down. His answers confused Nicodemus. Does that often happen in your life? We put Jesus in a box and all of a sudden we have to question what we know. When has that happened to you? When have you been confused by how the Spirit has moved in you or through the church? Ultimately, Jesus claims that the Spirit moves us to interpret God in ways that go beyond certitude. We don't need to know everything without a doubt, lest we find ourselves like Nicodemus, challenged in our thinking.

Nicodemus spoke of being "born again," but Jesus speaks of being "born from above." The Greek word for both is the same, one of several places in this passage that a word has dual meanings. Jesus claims that this rebirth is not a manipulation of the flesh, but a gift of the Spirit that blows where it will. The Spirit leads us to the waters of baptism, to the new life of a Christian, to a new understanding of Christian community. The Spirit leads us to an idea of a God who loves enough to give the world Jesus as Savior. The Spirit leads us to understand the Son of Man, crucified for humans to know love.

On this Trinity Sunday, this text is a rich example of our understanding of the unity of God we know in three ways. Even the Romans passage from the day refers to God who is Father, Son, and Spirit. The Isaiah passage is that same God we worship, one who is known by the prophet and would be known by Jesus and Paul. The reality of God who is God, Christ, and Spirit permeates the New Testament, inviting us to open our lives to the possibilities that are before us, the possibilities of a God who offers life eternal not to those who have the right answers, but to those who seek life.

Bringing the Text to Life

Like Nicodemus, we think we know God fully, only to be confronted with things that we don't know. The Trinity is one of those theological concepts that is hard to understand. Embrace that! There is mystery in our attempts to know God, and we with our finite minds can't fully understand who God is. There are several illustrations you can use to describe the Trinity, and all have their limitations: water, steam, and ice are all the same element but known in different ways. Or, an egg has three parts: shell, white, and yolk. My current favorite comes from a book called *3-in-1: A Picture of God* by Joanne Marxhausen.[3] This book shares the image of God as an apple: the peel, the flesh, and the seeds. Kids and adults alike can appreciate the teaching in the book.

You can use the symbolism of a hat. I wear three hats . . . or more. I am mom. I am wife. I am pastor. I am all of those things at the same time and can't stop being one when I am serving as the other. But underneath it all, I am Lynn. I am and I do all of those other things, but that doesn't change who I am at my core. The Trinity is much like that. God doesn't change who God is, but we can know God in different ways.

June 2, 2024–Second Sunday after Pentecost

1 Samuel 3:1-10, (11-20) and Psalm 139:1-6, 13-18; Deuteronomy 5:12-15
and Psalm 81:1-10; **2 Corinthians 4:5-12**; *Mark 2:23-3:6*

Cyndi McDonald

Preacher to Preacher Prayer

Dear God, sometimes I feel so ordinary. I cannot seem to make anything happen. I compare myself to others and wonder whether I am enough. Help me remember it is not about me. Dwell within. Shine your light of love, your power working within, to bring about more than I can ask or imagine. Amen.

Commentary

Paul bounces back. When the Corinthians question his authority, salary, and even his stature, Paul defends his choices, all the while tirelessly pointing to Jesus.

What keeps him going? What can we learn for those moments when we want to give up?

First, he embraces their criticism that there isn't much to him. Instead of drawing authority from his dramatic call story and telling about the light that blinded him on a Damascus road, Paul turns their attention to the one who said "let there be light." He is not a second Moses. It's not his face that shines with light! He claims to be nothing more than a common clay pot.

H. A. Williams suggests that laughter is the "purest" way to respond to God's acceptance.[1] To laugh at ourselves is an echo of God's genuine acceptance of us as flawed and imperfect beings. None of us are super-apostles or ultra-disciples. Instead of pretending we are perfect, can we not celebrate God's acceptance?

In improv comedy, the participant always says yes. Told, "You are a rabbit," the comedian begins to hop up and down. Told that he is not much of an apostle, Paul answers, "Yes, I'm just a common clay jar." Paul, who writes elsewhere to rejoice always (Philippians 4:4) and in every circumstance, understands that lightness and play are part of resiliency. Joy never depends on circumstances.

Second, Paul's confidence does not depend on the praise of the Corinthians or by external success. His worth depends on knowing the light of Christ who accepts Paul and dwells within Paul. Each criticism of Paul—he gets in trouble, he is confused—is greeted with a yes. And there is more. I'm knocked down but not knocked out. I'm harassed but never abandoned. The exterior isn't pretty but what's inside this clay jar never abandons me. God is with us.

Bringing the Text to Life

Imagine spending hours in the kitchen baking a cake, packing it in a simple cardboard box, and taking it to a birthday celebration. What if the recipient complained about the box? If instead of saying thank you, they say the cake must be worthless since it didn't arrive on a fancy platter.

Perhaps your church feels frustrated and belittled. Embrace the yes. We aren't Paul, who traveled throughout most of the known world. We haven't preached a sermon like Peter in which three thousand are converted. But the early church (and churches of today) is full of ordinary clay pots who are easy to overlook. And they were full of the light of Christ!

We need clay pots like Barnabas, who sees God at work in Paul when other church leaders see only a persecuting enemy. Who offers encouragement in your church?

We need clay pots like Tabitha. She couldn't feed a multitude with five loaves and two fish, but she could show the love of God by sharing what she owned. Who is the practical person who notices needs?

We need clay pots like Rhoda. As members of the church gather to pray for Peter's release from prison, she hears him knock on the door. She is treated like a crackpot, full of crazy ideas, but keeps on annoying those gathered until they go see for themselves. If not for Rhoda, they'd still be inside praying and Peter would still be outside knocking on the door. Who are the clay pots in your church?

I think of Bob, who was not someone that I thought about much as a youth. Bob was always available to help the church's youth group. We could count on him as a chaperone or driver. Bob didn't say much. But when we went on a mission trip, he brought extra tools and was there to hold a ladder.

When I thought of the youth program, I admired the leader with dynamic messages and the chaperone who always had a silly song for us to sing on the bus. We rolled our eyes, but sang along. And we even had fun. If I ever thought about Bob, I wondered why he hung around without saying much.

I forgot about Bob after high school. While I occasionally went to church on weekend visits home, I didn't think I had time for church. Or prayer. Or God.

Then I was in a department store, and Bob recognized me, and came over and started talking. How are you doing? Are you enjoying college? Have you found a church home? I don't think I'd ever heard Bob say that many sentences in a row.

Bob pulled an index card out of his pocket, and said, "I pray for you every Friday. I pray for everyone in your group on Fridays." The card was full of names for Monday, Tuesday, Wednesday . . . and Friday.

Bob was the clay pot. Ordinary and common. And his persistence and living grace encouraged me in a way I never expected. Who is your Bob?

How could you celebrate and help people see beyond the ordinary to the light of Christ shining within?

June 9, 2024–Third Sunday after Pentecost

1 Samuel 8:4-11, (12-15), 16-20, (11:14-15) and Psalm 138;
Genesis 3:8-15 *and Psalm 130; 2 Corinthians 4:13–5:1; Mark 3:20-35*

Cyndi McDonald

Preacher to Preacher Prayer

Everlasting and ever loving God, you never stop seeking. The Pentecost winds continue to blow, your spirit never giving up on us. Speak into our anxiety and shame, that we might respond to your grace with trust and obedience. Amen.

Commentary

The Genesis story is rich with possibilities, explaining much about the human condition and our brokenness in both vertical (with God) and horizontal (with one another) relationships. What a change to people created in the image of a trinitarian God. Instead of seeing themselves as one flesh, they hide from one another in shame. Adam answers God with blame of both the woman and God (who gave her to him). The consequences of fear and blame are hierarchy (Genesis 3:16) and objectification, as the man names Eve as he once named the animals (Genesis 3:20).

For the first time, someone human uses the word *I*: "I heard your sound in the garden; I was afraid because I was naked, and I hid myself" (v. 10).

God is not petty, watching and waiting with lightning bolts primed to strike instantly at the first hint of disobedience. There is time for them to attempt to arrange fig leaves into coverings. There is time to locate hiding places.

Thankfully, God who is the first mover of creation now makes the first move of redemption. God comes. God calls. This is how God will bring salvation, through incarnation, God with us.

How do you image God calling, "Where are you?" Is there gentleness? How will you convey the grace in this miracle that they live? God, the giver of life, seems to prefer giving to taking life, choosing not to track sins (Psalm 130:3). There are consequences to their disobedience, but God is not callous. God provides for their needs; this grace is costly, requiring animal skins to clothe them.

The goal of the game "hide-and-seek" is to be found eventually, either as the last of the hiders or by revealing oneself when the seeker calls out that they give up. Many of us have stories about the game. We've seen a child deliberately sticking a leg out in order to be found. Sometimes a hiding place is so good, the child cannot be found, and falls asleep while the whole family or neighborhood frantically searches.

The game doesn't always work out as expected because the players are fallible. Perhaps the person who is "it" isn't good at finding; they get distracted or tired and leave. There are many reasons not to trust the seeker.

These people who did not trust God enough to obey God's one command now must learn to trust the seeker. Jesus Christ will reveal what God is like: choosing to come as a vulnerable baby rather than an authoritarian ruler, choosing to embrace our pains and weeping with Mary and Martha. This is love so perfect that he offers himself on the cross on our behalf. There is no one more trustworthy. God's response to the cycle of asserting power over others is to lay down all power. God breaks cycles of blaming others by taking on all blame. God in the flesh reveals the perfect love that is trustworthy.

In Jesus Christ, we see how God mends both the vertical and horizontal relationships. Instead of our "solution" of independence, God calls people to live in the world as God's people. Jesus describes a new kingdom, a kin-dom, in which obedience to God identifies his true brothers, sisters, and mothers (Mark 3:20-35). The command to love God is paired with love of neighbor.

Where is the good news? It is in the one who calls out "where are you?"

Bringing the Text to Life

Christianity is no longer the cultural norm in many places. The hearer may be the only Christian in the workplace or extended family. They may be the one asked to explain the latest religious controversy or church conflict. But there is no need, like Adam and Eve, to hide in shame. Institutions and arguments reflect flawed people. The gospel is about Jesus, and always good news, and always trustworthy.

Where do you see the healing of the relationship with God leading to healing in relationships with others?

Consider using an extended reading to remind the hearers of the scripture's context. "Spill the beans" has a short and yet humorous retelling.[2] Or, use a Bible search to create a two-person reading in which people take turns using verses from the Psalms that include the word *trust*. Our song through the ages as God's people is one of trusting in the Lord.

A children's sermon could introduce Grover, the Sesame Street Muppet, who is fearful when he reads the title page of the book *The Monster at the End of the Book*.[3] There is a monster ahead! With each page he is desperate to avoid the book's end, trying to hide, asking the reader not to turn pages, and even nailing down pages so that they cannot be turned. At the end, he learns that the monster is lovable (it's Grover). What would it mean to recognize the grace in our story and its full ending, rather than to live in fear? To recognize that the perfect love of God is trustworthy and will cast out all fears? To respond to the grace of God's redemption not with fear, blame, or shame, but as those who are freed for joyful obedience.

June 16, 2024–Fourth Sunday after Pentecost

*1 Samuel 15:34-16:13 and Psalm 20; Ezekiel 17:22-24 and Psalm 92:1-4,
12-15; 2 Corinthians 5:6-10, (11-13), 14-17;* **Mark 4:26-34**

Cyndi McDonald

Preacher to Preacher Prayer

*Everlasting God, help us trust in the mystery of your ongoing work in these ordinary days.
Although the noisy Pentecost party streamers and balloons have been returned to boxes and
sacristies, we trust that the winds of the Holy Spirit continue to breathe life in our lives
and the church.*

Commentary

The parables of the farmer and the mustard seed both encourage hope. We can
trust that God, who once commanded the earth to bring forth plant life (Genesis
1:11), continues to be at work, bringing life in the planted seed. The farmer can sleep
without knowing exactly how this happens, only that that the creative energy of God
is both mysterious and trustworthy.

An anxious congregation may need reminding that God is still working in ways
we cannot observe. Too much worry is like constantly pulling back the soil to check
whether anything is happening, disturbing roots and arresting the development of
the seed. Do the work of cultivating, weeding, and watering, and trust that God is at
work in ways we cannot observe. (If you know any farmers, you also know that there
is always plenty to do during the waiting time!)

Your congregation may associate the mustard seed as a good thing full of potential. But Jesus's hearers may have heard this story differently. Mustard plants are
invasive and planting locations are restricted.[5]

Likely Jesus's hearers would prefer Ezekiel's parable of God taking a cedar tree
branch and placing it on a mountain in Israel, where the trunk sends out branches
and shelters birds of every kind (Ezekiel 17:22-24). Who wouldn't love to return

home from exile to become a glorious tall tree? While they are no longer in exile, they live in Roman occupation rather than as a strong nation.

Instead of God's restoration of a political kingdom, Jesus compares the Kingdom of God to a mustard bush. It's not even a tree! Thin branches sway with the wind, bouncing as birds land on them, seemingly not a reliable protective structure. Like the cedar tree, the mustard bush may shelter birds, but who wants such a scraggly structure?

Bringing the Text to Life

In *Leadership on the Line*, Ronald Heifitz and Marty Linsky argue that profound change is "more honest than grandiose," incremental, and built on enduring and orienting values.[5] The truth that we aren't a grandiose cedar tree may bring healing.

What truth could bring transformation? Perhaps this is celebrating the diversity within your congregation. Unlike a tree with a single trunk, a shrub has many stems that connect to the root. Diversity is like the branches that reach out in myriad directions theologically, politically, ethically, socially. How can God use these differences to reach outward?

The branches of the bush depend on one another. They lean on one another, protecting one another from harsh winds. How do the diverse members of your congregation support one another even as they rub against and chafe one another?

We had many differences in responding to COVID-19. One particularly outspoken family (the Smiths) scorned wearing masks and limiting gatherings. They offended a second family (the Browns) with at-risk family members, who saw this as a betrayal of caring for one another. Despite the grievances and hurt feelings, when the Smiths contracted a severe case of COVID-19 and were unable to work, the Browns galvanized the church. They brought meals and paid rent and utility bills to support people they had condemned. There was more to the church than met the eye. Deep roots of love prevailed. Emphasizing the values we have in common can overcome some of the chafing found in diversity.

We in the pulpit might need truth. Rather than focus on a grandiose vision or adopting programs replicating the success of "cedar tree" large growing churches, how might we nourish the mustard seeds already within our congregations? Have you seen a new pastor begin a ministry about which they are passionate . . . and then the ministry fades with the pastor's departure?

What if instead we trust in the soil and seeds that God provides in every particular community? If your church has developed mission, vision, and values statements, this is a great Sunday for reflecting on these. Remind the congregation of the unique soil (gifts and graces), the ways that these are cultivated, and where you may already see sprouts and even fruits.

The mustard seed suggests God sometimes works in ways that offend our sense of propriety. John Wesley could not imagine God working outside the physical structures of the Church of England. Yet he writes, "At four in the afternoon I *submitted to be more vile* and proclaimed in the highways the glad tidings of salvation" (italics mine).[6]

What would it mean to embrace a "more vile" method of ministry? To pray, "Lord, send us the people who no one else wants." Share a story of reaching out to those no one wants. The Reverend Jorge Acevedo describes God answering that prayer by sending people with addictions.[7] A mother describes her answered prayers when the student council noticed and invited to their table those sitting alone.[8]

June 23, 2024–Fifth Sunday after Pentecost

1 Samuel 17:(1a, 4-11, 19-23), 32-49; Psalm 9:9-20; 2 Corinthians 6:1-13;
Mark 4:35-41

Will Willimon

Preacher to Preacher Prayer

Lord, help us not to be afraid of today or tomorrow. Still the storms that rage around us. Speak to us a word that gives us confidence in you and your work in the world. Assuage our fears so that we might have new confidence in your power working in the world to bring all things toward you. Amen.

Commentary

This Sunday we don't have a story from Jesus; we have a story about Jesus. I want you to listen to this story as a revealing parable that has much to say to us about the kind of God whom we meet in Jesus Christ.

The shadows are lengthening, and it is growing dark. Jesus comes to his disciples with a weird invitation:

"Let's cross over to the other side of the lake."

They left the safety of the crowd and took Jesus with them in the boat. No sooner had they gotten out into the middle of the Sea of Galilee than a horrible storm arose. Waves were crashing over the side of the boat. It was taking on water and began to sink.

Where is Jesus during this terrifying ordeal? He is sleeping peacefully on a pillow in the boat!

The disciples wake him up screaming, "Teacher, don't you care that we're drowning?"

Jesus arises, rebukes the wind and the waves, and preaches to the lake, "Silence! Be still!" The wind and the waves settle down and there was a great calm.

Then Jesus turns to his disciples and has the nerve to ask them, "Why are you frightened? Don't you have faith yet?"

Mark says they were filled with awe and they ask one another, "Who then is this? Even the wind and the sea obey him!"

Who is this? Who is this Jesus? And who are we to be following him?

I want you to take those as the questions that will guide us in our reflections on this little story.

Note that this nighttime sail into the storm was Jesus's idea. Sorry if you thought that discipleship with Jesus would always be smooth sailing!

I know a young person who had a religious experience when she was a counselor at a summer camp. She gave her life to Christ. She was told at the time, by an adult leader, that if she gave her life to Christ that so many things that bothered her about herself and about other people would be fixed by her relationship with Christ.

She got back home at the end of summer. She showed up at her high school, said a little prayer, and asked Jesus to give her a wonderful junior year.

Didn't work out that way. Some of her friends just didn't understand her newfound Christian commitment. She was openly ridiculed by some of them at a party. "Look at Miss Christian!" they mocked. Some of her classmates were outright hostile. "What gives you the right to think you are better than me?" they asked. She tried to explain to them that she didn't feel that way at all, but she was unable to change their misunderstandings of the Christian way.

When the waves began to beat against the side of the boat and the boat began filling with water, and the disciples feared they are going down they cried out, "Teacher, don't you care that we're drowning?"

Jesus, do you care? Isn't that the question that is somewhere deep in your soul in your times of greatest distress? Isn't that the question that we want answered by God? Even if we don't have the courage to ask it, isn't that the question? We know that God is real, that God is powerful and creative. But does God care?

People sometimes make a big deal out of atheism. Does God exist? In my experiences, that's rarely the main question people have about God. The main question is that of the disciples: do you care?

And Jesus rises from his serene sleep on the cushion (interesting contrast between the placid sleep of Jesus and the wild terror of his disciples), rebukes the storm, just like he earlier rebuked the demonic forces that tortured some people. And the wind and the waves cease, leading the awestruck disciples to ask, "Who is this?"

Who is this that even the wind and the waves obey him? Who is this powerful figure who commands even the forces of nature?

But this time through this story I'm wondering if the disciples' question—Who is this?—maybe had a different twist. Remember, this nighttime sailing was Jesus's idea in the first place. Let's say that many of those disciples are a lot like us. Let's say that maybe they were attracted to Jesus by his powerful deeds of healing. They watched him rebuke the demons. Perhaps they enjoyed his teaching. His stories are entertaining, aren't they?

So, it was a bit of a jolt to have Jesus invite them to venture out, in the dark middle of the night, out onto a sea that quickly became angry, threatening them all with destruction.

Maybe that's why (and this is the speculation of someone who has been working with Jesus for a long time) they blurted out, "Who is this?" Who is this who takes his closest, best friends and puts them in mortal danger? Who is this who is fast asleep when we are battling the waves? Who is this who treats his students in this way?

Yes, Jesus cares but not always in the way we expected and wanted him to care. He cares by calling us, sometimes calling us to venture forth into the storm.

They thought that Jesus was the solution to all their problems only to find that Jesus cast them into the middle of problems they would never have had if they had not signed on with Jesus. They thought they knew all about God until Jesus began hurling at them his enigmatic stories that raised more questions than answers. Who is this?

When Jesus sees the terror of his disciples, he marvels that they don't have enough faith. What is faith? Maybe, in the light of this story, faith is the determination to stick with Jesus, to be following him, even when he leads you into a storm, even when you are fearful.

I want you to take this story of Jesus and his disciples on the sea in the storm as a parable of what it's sometimes like to have faith in Jesus.

Bringing the Text to Life

When we pastors care for our people by counseling them, we have a responsibility to establish and to name the peculiar ecclesial, christological context for our caring. As pastors, we don't offer them free floating, unattached "care." We offer them care in the name of Jesus. That means that sometimes our care must be connected with pastoral instruction, even moral correction.

Of course, there are times when ethical judgments need to be "bracketed" out of the conversation between pastor and parishioner, suspending judgment so that the pastor and the counselee can be free to examine the various dynamics of a situation in a relatively non-defensive way. But this must be a tactical suspension of pastoral judgment, not an overgeneralized principle that is applied to every person in every pastoral care situation.

Caring for people is something that most people try to do. Caring for people *in the name of Christ* is a much greater challenge.

June 30, 2024–Sixth Sunday after Pentecost

2 Samuel 1:1, 17-27; Psalm 130; 2 Corinthians 8:7-15; **Mark 5:21-43**

Will Willimon

Preacher to Preacher Prayer

Lord Jesus, we confess that for most days in our lives, we don't require much faith in you to make it through. We are sailing along. Life is good. We can handle most things that come our way. Yet there are other days when a storm comes up out of nowhere. Dark clouds gather. Life seems set against us. We are out of control, and there is nothing we can do to change the course of events. It's then that we reach out to you in faith. We ask you to come among us with healing power, to set right the things that we cannot in our own effort set right. While we admit that it's sad that we don't come to you when we are not desperate, and that it's predictable that we neglect our relationship with you until things are out of control, accept us as those who at least know that you are the answer to our prayers.

Commentary

The healings of Jairus's daughter and of the woman suffering from a hemorrhage are stories told in each of the Synoptic Gospels (compare Matthew 9:18-26 and Luke 8:40-56). Curiously, though Mark is usually our most concise Gospel, Mark's treatment of these stories is longer than the Synoptics, suggesting how very important these two episodes are for Mark's project.

Again, Jesus is near the sea with great crowds clustering around him. Let's walk through some of the moves throughout Mark's Gospel. Jesus appoints twelve disciples (Mark 3:13-19). Jesus has conflict with his family (Mark 3:20-35). Now there are a series of parables of the reign of God (Mark 4:1-34). Disciples in a storm at sea with the calming of the storm (Mark 4:35-41) was last Sunday's gospel. Then there's a healing of a demoniac (Mark 5:1-20). A woman healed and a young girl restored to life (Mark 5:21-43), this Sunday's gospel. Then Jesus goes home to Nazareth where he encounters rejection and unbelief (Mark 6:1-6). Jesus sends forth his disciples out in mission to preach and heal (Mark 6:7-13).

Crowds clamor after Jesus, hearing "what he was doing" (Mark 3:7); the unclean spirits hail him as "Son of God, but Jesus orders them to secrecy (Mark 3:7-12). Jesus is being stalked. Ten times the crowds are mentioned (see Mark 3:9, 20, 32; 4:1, 36; 5:21, 24, 27, 30, 31). Everybody is trying to figure out, "Who then is this?"

All of this sets the scene for a miraculous healing that is to occur.

The worried father "begs him repeatedly" (strange, the language repeats the pleadings of the demon, Legion, in the previous story, Mark 5:10) for the life of his "little daughter." The father pleads for help "that she may *be made well* and *live!*" (Mark 5:23 ESV). Jesus immediately "went with him," the crowd continuing to press on him.

Then comes a woman. She interrupts the story as we are told of her medical history. Her pleas join those of the father in begging for "salvation"—"If I touch even his garments, I will be made well" (Mark 5:28 ESV). Jesus asks rather accusingly, "Who touched me?"

She falls down before Jesus and tells the truth of what has happened to her, beseeching for healing. Her illness has defined her and kept her enslaved. Jesus speaks to her not as "woman" but as "daughter," one whose "faith" has "made her well" (that is, "saved" her). Jesus blesses her and bids her to leave in "peace" (*shalom*). Her healing is mentioned almost as an afterthought (Mark 5:34).

Suddenly a crowd arrives to say that the leader's daughter has died. One person is saved, elated; another faces death and sorrow: "Why even trouble the teacher any further?"

Jesus then gives encouragement, "Do not fear, only believe" (Mark 5:36 ESV).

Jesus takes the little girl by the hand and commands her "Arise" (same word as prelude to resurrection). The little girl is twelve years of age, and the woman has suffered a twelve-year illness. Make of that what you will.

We join the crowd in their amazement. Still, Jesus tells us not to tell anyone about what has happened here. Somehow, we must "stop being afraid" and try to "live by trust" in the coming of God's kingdom (Mark 1:14-15).

In the face of their resignation, Jesus proclaims, "Do not fear, only believe" (Mark 5:36). Or better, "Do not be fearful, but believing." The father is in great fear; Jesus invites him toward faith that dispels fear, to move from fear to trust.

Clearly, faith is at stake here. The woman is declared faithful by Jesus, "your faith has made you well"; Jairus is encouraged to keep faith, even in the face of death, "Do not fear, only believe." We are surely meant to ask ourselves, will we receive God's kingdom by faith, or will we doubt, laughing mockingly? Will we deny faith's power or respond to Christ in faith?

Question: why did Jesus tell his disciples not to tell anybody about these miraculous acts of compassion? I wonder if it was to underscore that he and his ministry mean more than miraculous acts of compassion. The story of Jesus begins with Jesus saying, "Follow me." There will be spectacular moments of healing and compassion, but even so noble an endeavor is not Jesus's main mission.

Bringing the Text to Life

One of my pastors in Alabama served faithfully an impoverished area of Birmingham. His parsonage had been robbed numerous times. Neighborhood drug dealers had threatened him.

"I need to get you out of here," said I. "Six years is too long. I'll look for a church in a place that's safer."

"Bishop," the pastor said, "thanks, but I'm fine. I'm not like you. Can't be poetic or come up with all those cute illustrations. All I can do is just drop a text on 'em and let God do the rest. I can only preach to folks who are going down the third time, people who are at the end of their rope and without hope. I'm not a good enough preacher to preach to folks who are not down and desperate."

Do some of my sermons fail because I'm attempting to trim good news for the lost and dying to the limitations of the self-satisfied, contented upper-middle class?

Perhaps there was a time when preaching needed to be beguiling; in a missionary situation, we must simply announce, as clearly as we can, the good news that challenges Christendom's comfortable alliances, attempting to get the story of Jesus right for the downcast and dying, who are apt to know good news when they hear it.

July 7, 2024—Seventh Sunday after Pentecost

2 Samuel 5:1-5, 9-10; Psalm 48; 2 Corinthians 12:2-10; **Mark 6:1-13**

Will Willimon

Preacher to Preacher Prayer

Lord Jesus, we give thanks for the freedom that we enjoy gathering to worship you. Preserve us from using our religious freedom as an occasion to be lax in our practice of discipleship. Forgive us when we get confused in our loves and loyalties and substitute anything (including our citizenship) for discipleship. That you commission and send people like us is a daunting prospect, Lord—and a joyful thing as well. We give you joyful thanks that you chose people like us, even in our limits and our inadequacies, to be your emissaries, your spokespersons, your assistants in your wondrous work. Give us the grace to witness to you well in our time and place. Amen.

Commentary

In this Sunday's Gospel, verses 1-6 of chapter 6 are a stand-alone segment. We do not hear the conclusion of this story, until a couple of weeks later in the lectionary when the return of the disciples is narrated in Mark 6:30. What we have this Sunday is two stories, one of Jesus's rejection at home by his own family and the other his sending out of his disciples. We probably can't do justice to both. I suggest that we focus mostly upon the sending of the disciples.

We wonder why Jesus is rejected by many in his own hometown in Mark 6:1-6. At first, he seems to be welcome there, but then in verses 2-3 things go sour. Earlier, in Mark 3:21, Jesus's own family think that Jesus has "gone out of his mind."

Still, there are those who follow Jesus, even though they may not fully understand him. These people are called disciples.

Throughout Mark's Gospel, a major concern is the identity of Jesus. "Who is this?" seems to be the question on everybody's mind—rulers, religious authorities, crowds, disciples, and family members can't figure out who he is or what he is up to. Of course, Mark is skillfully prodding us to ask the same question. If you've got doubts about Jesus, you are in a large company; even his own family was confused. On the other hand, if you believe in Jesus and have faith in him, congratulations, you are part of a happy minority: you know who he is.

Which brings us to Mark 6:7-13. We've seen the disciples only a few times in the immediately previous chapters in Mark's Gospel. Frankly, they have not been very impressive: in Mark 4, they are baffled by Jesus's parables, and at the end of the chapter Jesus says that they are full of fear and lack faith, causing them to ask, when he calms the storm at sea, "Who then is this?"

These are the group of dullards and incompetents whom Jesus now sends forth to preach repentance, heal the sick, and cast out demons?

It's enough to make one question Jesus's judgment! And yet, in Mark's sending forth, the church senses our founding document, its constituting moment, the justification for the church, the rationale for the presence of everybody in worship on Sunday.

Bringing the Text to Life

Here in church, with this morning's Gospel set before us, I propose that we reflect upon the founding of the Christian church. Because that is what I hear celebrated in this Sunday's Gospel from Mark 6. Let me put this in context: Jesus, as we have heard, appears to have been rejected by members of his own family. Though he and his teaching have attracted crowds, they turned against him.

And maybe that is part of the reason why Jesus turns toward a small group of ordinary people and commissions them to be his disciples, sending them forth to do the work that he has been doing:

> He called for the Twelve and sent them out in pairs. He gave them author-
> ity over unclean spirits. He instructed them to take nothing for the journey
> except a walking stick—no bread, no bags, and no money in their belts. . . .
> So they went out and proclaimed that people should change their hearts
> and lives. They cast out many demons, and they anointed many sick people.
> (6:7-13)

Jesus burst forth on the scene preaching that God's realm is coming near. He has been teaching about that coming kingdom. He performed signs and wonders to indicate that the time for a change of administrations has come. He is going head-to-head with the powers that be: religious, governmental, and demonic.

Now Jesus turns to these twelve ordinary people and calls them and sends them out into the world to do the very same things he has been doing. He is sending them out to proclaim and to call people to transformed living. He's sending them to go head-to-head with the demonic and to perform acts of healing.

This is a rather remarkable moment in the Gospel of Mark. Mark's Gospel begins with an introduction of Jesus as the long-awaited Messiah, the Son of God. With an opening acclamation like that, we expected some amazing signs and wonders.

But did we expect that the same Messiah, the Son of God, would then turn around and delegate his messianic, saving, world-transforming work to this group of ordinary people?

And by the way, as we have seen in Mark's Gospel, these disciples are very, very ordinary. They misunderstand Jesus from the very first. They never seem to get the point of his teaching. When Jesus performs some miraculous act, they seem as befuddled and baffled as the crowds who clamor after him.

Maybe you are thinking that Jesus has waited until the sixth chapter of the Gospel to call these disciples—vetting them, observing their behavior, discovering their talents until he was at last ready to call them.

Forget it. These disciples moved from dumb to dumber. They remain clueless, stumbling along after Jesus, all the way to the end of the Gospel. Mark seems to go out of his way to demonstrate that the reason they were chosen to be disciples is not their gifts, their talent.

And I am saying that we are to watch closely because what we are seeing here, in Jesus calling to himself and sending out from himself these twelve, we are seeing the birth of the church. Our founding as God's people. This scene ought to be the equivalent of the church's constitutional convention.

This story is the rationale for why we are gathered here this Sunday. In fact, even though you may not have been consciously aware of it, this story of Jesus calling and sending of the disciples explains why you are here this morning. Those first disciples are the precursors for all of us.

I'm sorry if you thought that God works solo. Maybe you thought that because God is omnipotent and omniscient, God does anything God wants all by God's self. This God who comes to us as Jesus Christ calls ordinary people to work with him. Jesus, the great delegator. The Savior who chooses not to save the world by himself.

July 14, 2024–Eighth Sunday after Pentecost

2 Samuel 6:1-5, 12b-19; *Psalm 24; Ephesians 1:3-14; Mark 6:14-29*

Vidalis Lopez

Preacher to Preacher Prayer

We enter your holy place, seeking to worship you in truth. Transform us, help us, equip us with your wisdom and grace to know your will for us. It's easy to seek our preferred way and alternative motives. Examine our heart. Enlighten our mind. In this ordinary season, may the spirit of Pentecost continue to inspire our spirit. Kindle a global revival of empathy, justice, and peacemaking. Let us discern your guidance and abide in you.

Commentary

In 2 Samuel 6:1-5, 12b-19, David dances like nobody is watching, or like someone *is* watching. David and all of his people set out to move the ark of God to Jerusalem. David celebrates in the Lord's presence with all his strength. The narrator repeatedly notes David's accomplishments. Second Samuel 5:10 (ESV) says, "And David became greater and greater, for the LORD, the God of hosts, was with him." Victory over enemies, joyful celebrations, stewardship of the ark and distribution of food to the people were evidence of God's favor and blessing over David, a warrior king.

It is important to recognize that the selected verses don't tell the whole story. In verses 6-11, Uzzah helps carry the ark. He touches it as he attempts to adjust it and prevent harm against it. Yet, Uzzah dies after doing that. David reacted with anger and expressed fear. He said, "How can the ark of the LORD come into my care?" (v. 9 NRSVUE). David rerouted the ark's placement, laying it in the house of Obed-edom. After three months, King David was informed of how the Lord blessed Obed-edom's household because the ark rested there. David, then, went and reclaimed the ark.

How is it fair for Uzzah to die trying to stabilize the ark? This is to many readers a disturbing part of the story. God seems harsh. Second Samuel 6 also includes Michal's resentment toward David. Before Michal is judged harshly, we should remember she loved David, her husband. She saved his life (1 Samuel 18–19), and yet she could not bear children. David had children with other wives, and her father Saul's reign was over. This selected lectionary passage concludes with verse 19 indicating that all the people after celebrating and eating went home. Michal, however, was home watching from the outside looking in.

It's unclear whether David's priestly garments were worn inappropriately. The text says that David dressed in a linen priestly vest as he danced, jumped, and sacrificed burnt offerings. Perhaps he celebrated like no one was watching and everyone saw him free-spirited.

Can there be anything flawed and unholy in God's mysterious and sacred presence? We can wonder about all the circumstances and movements happening around the ark of God, the Lord's holy presence, but we see it as clear as mud. David sees how the Lord can burst out against the Philistines (5:20), as well as within Israel. We can wonder about all the circumstances and movements happening around the ark of God, the Lord's holy presence. We can see what is clear as mud. We can see flaws, a political and influential leader's unclear motive, use and misuse of power, resentment toward family, hypocrisy, fear, and anger. This passage invites us to explore how God's infinite wisdom and promised faithfulness can be sought by humans with either an honest willingness or desire for self-glory, or both, or manipulation. We can't be sure if David's motives are founded in gratitude or self-gratification, or both. Perhaps we are to reflect on how humanity wrestles with both, often simultaneously. David was not all bad, nor all good, but he was clearly in need of God's ongoing transformational presence. Most people resonate with that tension. Sin is real, faith is real. The narrative leaves room for both readings.

Who then shall stand in God's holy presence? (Psalm 24:3b). All of life's realities can draw us to recognize our need for God's holy presence. We see how God remains near and able.

How do we enter God's presence? Who stipulates it as justified or not? A binary lens can limit our way of understanding how God's grace works through gray areas, unclear or unresolved heart matters. The spiritual gift of discernment and accountability can heal our lives in community. God's amazing faithfulness is evident through and despite us.

Bringing the Text to Life

Some people cheer for Disney World's celebrations and parades, while some suspect the organizations' true motivations. Peaceful marches and protests for social change are a source of hope and courage for many people. While for others, protests are an offense to our nation's history and traditions. Our nation has been enduring a divisive political climate. Leaders attempt to lead us toward victory with their own take of who is right and who is wrong. Do leaders win to care or care to win? Celebrations, campaigns, and movements may offer possibilities and risks. Innocent people may be criminalized or treated lesser than; guilty people may be acquitted.

Is anyone with fault capable of having a change of heart? We can feel so many emotions that affect how we trust God's will and others with whom we interact. What has happened in our churches and communities that has led to division, distrust, and disdain? We can see how the spiritual gift of discernment is needed in the community of faith. When and how do we recognize this spiritual gift as much as we applaud other gifts and achievements?

We struggle to understand the motives and actions observed in this text, yet God remains present. In times of crisis, people are drawn to one another to pray, lament, and serve together. For self-identifying Christians and to anyone curious enough to consider, the sacrament of Holy Communion can serve as the most loving invitation into a safe space where holiness reveals abundant grace, love, forgiveness, compassion, mercy, and hope.

Take time to identify the practices in the church community where God's holy presence is embraced and can be extended into our everyday imperfect lives.

July 21, 2024–Ninth Sunday after Pentecost

2 Samuel 7:1-14a; Psalm 23; **Ephesians 2:11-22;** *Mark 6:30-34, 53-56*

Vidalis Lopez

Preacher to Preacher Prayer

We enter your holy space needing you. These aren't ordinary times. May the power of hostility in our world today only deepen our yearning for true peace, for you, Jesus Christ. The Holy Spirit has come. Renew our hearts, mind, and spirit. Amen.

Commentary

In the Pauline letter of Ephesians 2:11-22, the church receives substantial affirmation of how Christ dwells in the church and intends for the church to be instrumental to the divine plan of salvation. The author begins chapter 2 highlighting God's cosmic salvific work for the Gentiles who are growing the church. God is rich in mercy. He brought us to life with Christ while we were dead because of those things that we did wrong. You are saved by grace! (2:4-5). The first ten verses include a contrast between life "before and after" God's intervention.

The selected lectionary passage follows with an inference of how Jews and Gentiles are to build and advance the church's movement as God intended. The author recaptures the historical and cultural significance of circumcision, an Abrahamic covenant that set apart the Israelites as God's people. Gentiles were the uncircumcised, meaning without God, unsaved (vv. 11-13).

The circumcised and uncircumcised were two separate groups within the human race, yet the church in Ephesus is growing by integrating Gentiles. It was puzzling to believe that a community of faith could thrive with historical and seemingly foundational differences. The author interlaces a cultural and relational evolvement with a greater cosmic transformational change.

Even though verses 14-16 point to peace, first-time listeners may have experienced collective upheaval. The baptismal/covenant prescription was being transformed through Christ into an expanded identity through integration by unity over uniformity. This revolutionary change is evident not only in those who were once considered outsiders, but for those who belonged first or by birthright.

It's important to remember Jesus was sentenced to death by the governing powers of the time. A Jewish high priest as well as a Roman (non-Jew) were involved in the unjust violence against Jesus. Everyone means everyone. For all have sinned and fall short of God's glorious standards (Romans 3:23). However, with Jesus's death and resurrection, the hostility to God ended (v. 16). God canceled the hostility with the most generous gift of hospitality, a powerful reconciliation.

When Jesus was interrogated by Pilate (John 18:33-36), Pilate pointed out how he was not a Jew and how the chief priests of Jesus's nation handed Jesus over to him. When Pilate asks Jesus what he had done, Jesus replied, "My kingdom doesn't originate from this world. If it did, my guards would fight so that I wouldn't have been arrested by the Jewish leaders. My kingdom isn't from here" (v. 36).

This text, when misread, can deduce that either Jews or Gentiles, or both, were supposed to eradicate either their culture, race or customs, or all of these, altogether by creating a new humankind/non-race (v. 19). Without careful consideration, this kind of reasoning can promote anti-Semitism or cultural assimilation. Is Judaism meant to be abolished here? Is this Pauline letter implying that we should say, "I am a former Jew, former Irish, or former Puerto Rican?" No. The overarching biblical narrative upholds the command to love one another as thyself, avoiding a hierarchical-configured love.

Verses 17-22 point to an emphasis on integration, "You are fellow citizens with God's people" (v. 19). Through Jesus Christ as the cornerstone, all nations (far away and near) may belong in God's household. By being reconciled with God, we are reconciled to one another.

Bringing the Text to Life

What does it mean to be saved? According to this Pauline letter, reconciliation is an act of salvation. The power of God's reconciliation converts the way churches are founded. Cultural, social, and religious divisions are contrary to God's vision of human salvation.

Statements like "I don't see color or race" or "talks about race and social tensions must be prohibited in church" have been gaining more airtime in our country. The increasing polarization in politics has raised the temperature so high that careful reading and reflection of this text challenges people's comfort levels. Yet, the good news belongs in our churches more than ever. Separation as a way of avoidance does not solve the problem because it makes reconciliation impossible.

Jesus's selfless act challenges privatized or solitary salvation (like the idea of "save yourself" or "save your ticket for entry into eternity"). Growing faith does not make things comfortable or easier, but holier and truer. God's reconciliation redeems humanity from its inherited brokenness. God's salvation welcomes us into God's fold, so that the body of Christ, the church, can extend the gracious hospitality for people to connect with God, belong to a community, and build God's kingdom on earth (2 Corinthians 5).

Affirming together the Nicene Creed: "We believe in one holy catholic and apostolic church" can underline the value of the creeds passed on from one generation to the next.

Encouraging and experiencing an interfaith service is a palpable approach to practicing hospitality and can be a witness to how connected we can be by communicating our shared values.

Challenging the church to engage in difficult and uncomfortable Bible studies to understand the existing social and racial tensions can be an act/process of discipleship. Discomfort and avoidance lead to mistrust, thus, dissociation among people. Dorothee Soelle, a German political theologian, was haunted by the Holocaust. She wrestled with the question, *How do we speak of God after Auschwitz?*

The new household of God is a transformed church. Sunday gatherings are not a weekly "time out" from reality. This is a counterfeit "peace." How can we as the church deepen our trust in the power of Christ's reconciling saving grace?

July 28, 2024–Tenth Sunday after Pentecost

2 Samuel 11:1-15; 2 Kings 4:42-44; Ephesians 3:14-21; **John 6:1-21**

Vidalis Lopez

Preacher to Preacher Prayer

Gracious God, I'm in awe of how you are the way out of no way. When it may seem like trying times do not subside or end but become the norm, I pray that you receive my near-sighted longings and transform them to make a banquet table of hope. Remind me by the example of many leaders' steadfast faith and your gracious presence that you are always with me as my guide. Amen.

Commentary

The Gospel of John focuses on revealing Jesus's christological identity. From the outset, Jesus embodies the power of God. Jesus is Christ the Lord. In the beginning was the Word, the Word was with God, and the Word was God (John 1). This selected lectionary passage is not essentially about how bread miraculously appeared to feed five thousand hungry people. Jesus acts in ways for the people and disciples to encounter a self-revealing God. Jesus's walking on water (vv. 16-21) portrays the power of Jesus's presence while confronting fear. Jesus is who Jesus says he is, "I am." Throughout the Gospel of John, witnesses are in awe of Jesus's miracles. So much so that they wish to appoint Jesus as king. But earthly empires fall and die in due time. This biblical narrative is written so that Jesus is known as the Messiah who raises an evolving and resilient faith in all who choose to believe.

A large crowd followed Jesus because they had seen him perform miracles (vv. 1-2). The disciples and Jesus were gathering when they noticed the crowd approach them. The dialogue that follows between Jesus and two disciples, Philip and Andrew, is described as a test of faith (v. 6). This account compares notably to an Old Testament narrative. In 2 Kings 4:38-44, the prophet Elisha gathered with a group of prophets. At that time, there was a famine in the land. The story unfolds with Elisha's miraculous feeding of one hundred people with just twenty loaves of barley bread.

The man who brought the little amount of food to Elisha came from Baal-shalishah. It's worth noting that this implies the man associated with pagan worship (to Baal). There was an ongoing contest in Israel's ancient history between Yahweh and Baal. John 6:14 specifies how the multitude who witnessed Jesus's miracle professed Jesus as the prophet coming into the world.

John's Gospel logs Jesus attending six festivals in Jerusalem. Passover was soon to be celebrated (v. 4). This segment compares to Moses's intercessory work marking the first Passover. When Moses leads the people through the wilderness, hunger strikes several times. Moses asks God, "Where am I to get meat for all these people?" (Numbers 11:13). Jesus, on the other hand, knew exactly what to do, setting himself apart from any prophet.

The crowds and even the disciples seem relieved to see Jesus as an extraordinary prophet like Moses and Elisha. But they all struggled to see beyond that. Verse 15 unveils how Jesus understood that the people were going to insist that he become their king and resolve once and for all their existing troubles. For that reason, Jesus took refuge, leaving the scene.

Later that day, when it was dark, Jesus reappeared to the disciples who were in a boat three or four miles deep in rough water. Jesus approached them walking on water and introduced himself saying, "I Am. Don't be afraid" (vv. 16-20).

There is a self-disclosing theme developing throughout the Gospel of John.

John 2:13-23 discloses how leaders question Jesus after he overturned tables at the temple. "By what authority are you doing these things?" (v. 18)."What miraculous sign will you show us?" Jesus's response pointed to his death and resurrection. John 3 includes the encounter of Jesus and Nicodemus, a Pharisee, who acknowledged Jesus as a reputable teacher.

John 4:19-26 covers Jesus's conversation with the Samaritan woman at Jacob's well. She said, "Sir, I see that you are a prophet." The conversation becomes a transformational encounter for the woman when Jesus reveals his identity, saying, "I Am —the one who speaks with you."

John 5 describes Jesus healing a man on the sabbath. Consequently, Jesus is harassed by some of the religious leaders. Then, in an intense exchange of words between Jesus and the leaders, Jesus said in John 5:24, "I assure you that whoever hears my word and believes in the one who sent me has eternal life and won't come under judgment but has passed from death into life."

Bringing the Text to life

Salvation comes through Jesus who says, "I am the way and the truth and the life. No one comes to the Father except through me" (John 14:6 NIV). Crowds followed Jesus because they saw his miracles as the solution to their present troubles. It is part of our human nature to become more focused on our immediate needs rather than trusting God for the bigger picture God has in mind. When we encounter Jesus, we can expect something. But what is it that we expect? How can God's signs be considered windows or steps toward the Savior/salvation?

This reading depicts Jesus as mightier than other prophets. Moses and Elisha were amazing leaders called by God, but they were never saviors. No human, no political leader can offer everlasting restoration and salvation. Seeking God's glory is more important than our transient wins.

Picture yourself standing alone in a dark room. Imagine hearing a wooden door creaking open and you can't see who is coming in. The sound of footsteps follows and you do not know who it is. Then, a voice of someone you recognize (and appreciate) breaks the silence and says, "It's me." You know exactly who that is, and you can finally catch your breath.

How can we today describe dark times in our society, families, and in our churches, provoking fear within us or among us? How do we turn to God in times of need? How can remembering the miracles of the past reassure us today?

Many churches across denominational lines face financial challenges or lack committed people to serve as volunteers. How do we respond and stay the course as our collective faith faces hardships? The presence of Jesus Christ in our lives is peace, salvation, and hope. Jesus is our Lord and Savior through both miracle and simple presence.

August 4, 2024–Eleventh Sunday after Pentecost

*Exodus 16:2-4, 9-15; Psalm 78:23-29; Ephesians 4:1-16; **John 6:24-35***

Cynthia D. Weems

Preacher to Preacher Prayer

God of all creation, give us the words to draw people more deeply into relationship with you. When we want a quick solution or miracle to fill us up, slow us down to allow for a deeper understanding of you.

Commentary

In this passage we find a crowd of people who have been fed. The story of the multiplication of the loaves and fish is just a few verses before this one in John's Gospel. This crowd is not only fed but fed miraculously. Their stomachs aren't quite empty yet and before they get empty, they want to find out who this Jesus is and from where that food came.

Jesus is no dummy and he knows the human heart and the human stomach. He surely was not surprised that human beings in human bodies would want to follow the source of miraculously obtained food. Yet Jesus also knew the people were hungry for more than just food for their stomachs. He knew their souls were as hungry as their bellies. Just as they were looking for more bread, they were looking for more life—a spiritually sustaining life that would allow them to rise from that perpetual feeling of emptiness to a permanent feeling of belonging.

Jesus then gives us one of the most beautiful "I am" statements in scripture, "I am the bread of life" (v. 35). Through "I am" statements in the Gospel of John, Jesus claims his divinity. God referred to himself as "I am" when Moses asked for an identifier at the burning bush. In Hebrew, the words for Lord are *I am*. When Jesus makes seven "I am" statements in the Gospel of John he is claiming his divine identity.

One could argue that the crowds got a couple of different surprises in these moments with Jesus. First, in looking for Jesus of Nazareth they actually found God. Then, in looking for bread for their stomachs, they found bread for their souls. Interestingly, they were not sure that's what they wanted. They seemed to be getting more than they bargained for. We are often not in a state of mind to recognize and rejoice in the fullness of the "I am."

What the people appear to want are "signs" or "works" of God. They liked what they saw before with the trick of turning a few loaves and fish into a mountain of food. They want to see more. They've heard many stories about God's miracles, like the manna in the wilderness. But Jesus attempts to get their thinking away from the signs and miracles. He says, "This is the work of God, that you believe in him whom he has sent" (6:29 ESV). The problem is this: true belief requires a different view of the world and this shift in worldview takes time. As a preacher, encouraging your listeners to lean into the depth of this passage and the requirement to fundamentally change worldviews is a key to unpacking the larger meaning of this scripture and the other "I am" statements that follow.

Those listening to a sermon about this text will want to know what exactly the belief is that Jesus is referring to. What is the belief that makes it possible to "never be hungry and never be thirsty"? It is the fundamental belief that God has sent to earth a son named Jesus to save an otherwise broken world. His is the body that will be broken in order to make eternal amends with the world. Believing that God loves the world so much that he sent his own son to save it is what essentially changes your view of the world. You see things differently. For God so loved the world, my problems aren't what I thought. For God so loved the world, I do not have to take on what is not mine. For God so loved the world, I can live and love freely. For God so loved the world, I can give generously. For God so loved the world, I can confidently share my heart, my stuff, my life.

For those who will celebrate the sacrament of Holy Communion on this Sunday, consider asking the listeners to look more closely at the bread. Look at the bread, about to be broken. Jesus wanted the world to be whole, but it could only get there through his broken limbs. The meal the disciples shared with him would fundamentally shift their view of the world. But the shift must be renewed, and that is why we come to the table. There is no special work or sign. "I am the bread of life," Jesus says. Receive this bread, believe it and you will live.

Bringing the Text to Life

There are many fun images of bread that play into what is at work in this passage. Ask the listeners to consider all the different types of bread: a French baguette, a sourdough loaf, a piece of pita, a slice of rye. Just as they imagine all the kinds of bread that exist in a supermarket aisle, Jesus tells them that he is the Bread of Life. What a surprise! The surprise continues as Jesus shares more. The people want a quick sign or miracle, something more like a Subway sandwich or fast food. Jesus is preparing a gourmet, sit-down meal, filled with conversation and relationship. This is a meal that will transform our lives. Are we ready for this kind of relationship with Jesus?

August 11, 2024–Twelfth Sunday after Pentecost

*1 Kings 19:4-8; Psalm 34:1-8; **Ephesians 4:25-5:2**; John 6:35, 41-51*

Cynthia D. Weems

Preacher to Preacher Prayer

Lord of joy and life, help me to speak into a passage that also challenges my spirit. I, too, can be impatient, angry, difficult. Allow me to hear Paul's words today so that I may share with honesty the challenges to living an obedient life. May my preaching words reflect my own journey toward a closer relationship with you and with others.

Commentary

"We are parts of each other in the same body," Paul writes in the second portion of verse 25. This may bring us comfort and it may cause panic! Being called to live in relationship with one another can be as comforting as a warm blanket—we belong to one another and are woven together. Yet this image can also be as suffocating as a blanket that is suddenly too warm, too tightly wrapped, too heavy. Living as one body implies that our relationships are an intimate part of our spiritual journey toward knowing and loving God. We are not called to compartmentalize our spiritual lives or our relationships. They are a part of the same package.

Yet, we are all aware of the many issues that come with relationships. Relationships are complex. N. T. Wright states in his book *Simply Christian*, "We all know we are made to live together, but we all find that doing so is more difficult than we had imagined."[1] Parents, siblings, spouses, friends, and coworkers all come with a complex array of beauty and trouble.

The context of Ephesus was no different. Paul was writing to a group of people familiar with the pains of living together in a complex community of social, economic, gender, and racial relationships. Paul's hope was to give the community some key concepts to focus on as they formed themselves in this new set of relationships within the body of Christ. These concepts are kindness, compassion, and forgiveness with a desire to imitate Christ.

Paul gives us this list of behaviors and practices that will keep us plugged in to our true source of life: God. This is because Paul considers our connection to God the only way we can stay true to any human relationship. What behaviors will keep us true to God? Putting away falsehood, speaking the truth, speaking truth in love, sharing words that give grace, being kind, being tenderhearted, being forgiving. Once when leading a Bible study on this passage the participants in the group named the following daily practices that helped keep them faithful to their relationships and pointed in the right direction: prayer, communication, understanding, and listening. People tend to have a general idea of what will keep them, and their relationships, out of trouble. Paul wants to codify this in our hearts as a reminder that what God wants for us is actually good for us and for those in relationship with us.

The trouble is, all of these are good suggestions and all of them are worth a try. But have you ever tried your hardest to model this kind of behavior in a relationship, only to find it still a sour, uncomfortable, and trying experience? We can work as hard as we can, as faithfully as we can, and still feel the effects of misunderstanding and pain. When reading Paul's letters that so often lift up the community and emphasize the importance of Christian community, it is also important to step back and remember that the behaviors he describes must begin with the individual in order for them to extend to the community.

I served a church once where a husband-and-wife team served as the choir director and organist, respectively. They were both very accomplished on the piano and often played piano four hand pieces. They played these pieces beautifully. I once joked with them about how many hours they must spend practicing together and they responded in a way that surprised me. They explained that in order for them to play the four hand pieces well, they both had to have practiced the piece individually with ease and near perfection in order to be prepared to play the piece well together.

We are each only as strong in relationship as we are as individuals. Paul knew that unless people were plugged into their creator, they couldn't very well plug into other relationships in healthy ways. This scripture passage is a reminder of the importance of the personal and the communal.

Bringing the Text to Life

Like the prior piano four hand example, consider asking your listeners to imagine a particular relationship in their lives. While imagining this relationship, ask them to consider what practices they engage in that prepare them to be in a healthy relationship with this person. Perhaps the person is an elderly parent who requires a significant portion of patience in order to address the challenges that come with aging and changing personalities. If so, what practices help the person to prepare to engage that relationship as faithfully as possible? Is it talking with others about how to care for aging parents? Is it prayer and meditation to center oneself before a visit? Is it learning from others who have experienced a similar family dynamic?

Consider other relationship with siblings, spouses, or coworkers. What are the practices that a person can do individually in order to make them a better, healthier participant in the relationship? How can we prayerfully enter each relationship with our best and healthiest self?

August 18, 2024–Thirteenth Sunday after Pentecost

1 Kings 2:10-12; 3:3-14; *Psalm 34:9-14; Ephesians 5:15-20;*
John 6:51-58

Cynthia D. Weems

Preacher to Preacher Prayer

O Lord, we pray this day for wisdom. We pray for it with humility, steadfastness, and a bit of desperation as we move toward another sermon, another conversation, another opportunity to share you with our flock. Give us wisdom this day, that it might be the foundation upon which our ministry rests.

Commentary

In this week's passage we find Solomon, son of David, paying a visit to Gibeon, outside of Jerusalem. While there, he sleeps in the sanctuary and hopes for a dream of divine revelation. Just this image gives a preacher the opportunity to examine with listeners the importance of putting ourselves in a place where we can truly listen for God's voice. How often do we do that? How often do we prioritize the quiet, peaceful setting that will allow us to truly seek God's voice? This is where Solomon begins and it is not an insignificant point. Spend some time with this element of the passage before jumping too quickly to the next (and most popular) portion of the passage.

Solomon sleeps, dreams, and then the Lord comes to him. The voice of God is heard and God asks Solomon what he wishes for. What a convenient time for God to arrive! We learn that Solomon set his heart on seeking God, put himself in a place where he might hear God, and then God appears. The Bible does not present this set of events as circumstance or coincidence. Solomon was ready and God showed up.

Solomon answers God's question. He asks for a "discerning mind." We would call this wisdom. Solomon asks for wisdom to serve God's people faithfully. In Hebrew, this is translated "a listening heart." What Solomon most wants is for God to give him a heart and mind that is continually open to the leading of God's spirit. What Solomon most wants is for the attitude of his visit to the sanctuary and his mindfulness and patience for God's voice to be ever present in his leading of the people of Israel. Solomon wants to emulate the mind and heart of God as closely as possible. This was an unexpected request. This was a request of the heart. And this request was granted.

The moment shared between Solomon and God is pivotal. It is pivotal because Solomon, already a young king and with the potential to be full of pride and conceit, acknowledges who is in charge of his life and his reign. In this request, Solomon humbles himself before God. He even says as much when he responds to the Lord's question. Solomon acknowledges that he is young and inexperienced and "[knows] next to nothing" (3:7). In this request, the Lord recognizes Solomon's true character. He recognizes Solomon as a person worthy of wisdom, and more.

James Harnish writes when assessing Solomon's life, "Biblical wisdom is not the accumulation of information; that's knowledge. Biblical wisdom is knowing what to do with the knowledge we acquire."[2] Solomon anticipated the challenges that would come to his reign as king. He knew he could hold all knowledge, wealth, and status and still not be the king he hoped to be. What he most desired was wisdom, a wisdom that would make him worthy of the title of king.

Solomon knew that all gifts were from God. Wisdom wasn't something he was either born with or could develop. Wisdom was a gift God would need to provide. This fits with the ancient understanding of both spiritual and material possessions—the Lord gifts them all. Nothing can be acquired or obtained without the Lord's initiation and this passage is no different. The Lord asks the question, Solomon makes the request.

The Lord also knew Solomon had many options for what he could have asked for. This is what happens when God takes a leap and asks what you want! Solomon could have asked for any number of things: wealth, power, possessions, an obedient people, a peaceful life. Yet Solomon asked for wisdom and the Lord was pleased. This gift of wisdom would bring other gifts to the people because it is a virtue that inspires other virtues. Wisdom will enable the people of Israel to live into the promises of their God. They will be more faithful because their leader seeks faithfulness in his leading. They will prosper because their leader is focused in the right direction and seeks to lead with integrity.

The preacher may want to conclude the sermon where it began, in the sanctuary with Solomon waiting for God. What does it mean to live deeply into a passage of scripture that reminds us that God seeks us out, comes and finds us, and will speak to us if our lives and hearts make room for God's voice. The Lord comes to us as the Lord came to Solomon and asks, "What can I give you?"

Bringing the Text to Life

Consider the hymn "Seek Ye First." It offers profound insight into today's passage and how we might live lives that seek the first and best things. Isn't this what God honored by granting Solomon his wish? God honored Solomon's desire to seek the things of God first as he led the people faithfully. When we wake up each morning, our thoughts, actions, and decisions can go in many directions. All directions start with each of us seeking something—an outcome, a reward, an accomplishment, a contribution. What if we begin by seeking the things of God and God's kingdom? How might that simple adjustment alter the remainder of what lies before us and the attitude and intention we take into each decision?

August 25, 2024–Fourteenth Sunday after Pentecost

1 Kings 8:(1, 6, 10-11), 22-30, 41-43; Psalm 84; Ephesians 6:10-20;
John 6:56-69

Jennifer Forrester

Preacher to Preacher Prayer

Gracious God, in the great mystery of it all, if we believe that you created everything from nothing, if we believe that you came to us all to live among us as your Son, then help us to believe the great mystery of it all. Help us to believe that you are indeed the bread of life, a bread that not only can sustain us but also strengthen us to live as you teach us to live on this earth. Amen.

Commentary

This is a tough and perhaps confusing scripture for us to hear living in the twenty-first century. The theme of Jesus being the bread of life is seen throughout the sixth chapter of the Gospel of John beginning with thousands who are hungry and fed on the lawn. But here, when we get to our verses today, when Jesus begins referring to the bread being the *living bread . . .* the flesh of Jesus, the scripture becomes even more difficult and perhaps even grotesque. Even the disciples said it was harsh in verse 60. It is harsh or difficult for us because it is a language we no longer speak, and it was harsh for the disciples because Jesus was breaking Levitical law by suggesting they drink blood. Drinking blood was forbidden because just as it was essential to the life of any living creature, it was sacred to God. However, this would have been a familiar idea for them, even if they were walking away offended.

In ancient sacrifice, when an animal was brought to the altar, only a portion was actually burned, even though the entire animal was being offered. A portion was always kept out for consumption by the priest, as a rule, and part to those who were worshipping. It was a feast of sorts, and with God as the guest of honor, once it was offered to God it was believed that God entered the flesh, hence when anyone ate it, they were literally eating God. When the feast was over and the worshippers left, they therefore left God-filled.

Jesus was challenging the disciples, though, because he knew that there were many that did not yet believe that Jesus was the way to eternal life. If they did not believe it for themselves, Jesus knew there would be no way for them to continue with him, and, besides, who would believe in Jesus as the way to eternal life if his disciples did not believe? They understood what Jesus was saying because they understood ancient culture. The problem was that they couldn't accept it. And that's where we meet this scripture even today. Intellectually we can understand the words of Jesus; however, morally the demands are just too high. Jesus knew there would be those who would betray him, even today. Jesus knows this because at the heart of it all there is a great mystery, and just like the disciples, we like to be able to explain everything. The truth is, there is no explaining how God is at the heart of it all.

Like all scripture, we need to understand the context so we can better understand what Jesus was trying to tell the disciples about the great mystery of his life and how, through it, they too have eternal life. As do we.

Bringing the Text to Life

Every time I read this scripture, I am reminded of a communion story a dear friend of mine shared with me about her First Communion in the Roman Catholic Church. If you recall, the Catholic tradition believes in transubstantiation, the idea that the Eucharist elements, the bread and wine or juice, convert to the actual body and blood of Christ upon consecration.

The day came for Jane's First Communion, only it wasn't completely joyous to start with because Jane's mom had left two weeks before, leaving Jane and her sister with their father. Jane was young, probably six or seven, and as you can imagine she had been struggling since her mom had left. Jane's dad, being a devout Catholic, insisted that they go ahead with the day, which is typically a celebration. Jane's aunt had come over to help Jane get ready. Everyone was trying to make her First Communion perfect. There were even presents and cake. When the time came, Jane walked up with the other children who were also receiving their First Communion. As the story goes, when it was Jane's turn to receive Communion, and the priest said this is the body and blood of Christ, Jane gasped as she looked at the icky chalice and turned and ran as fast as she could out of the church. In fact, she ran all the way home without her family. When her family finally caught up with her, Jane was upstairs in her room crying. Her father was so disappointed in her because she had denied Jesus that he took all of her presents back and threw her cake away. Needless to say, Jane never went back to church until her child was about that same age, six or seven, and part of an after-school program that was held at a United Methodist Church.

I think, like Jane, we don't always understand the mystery of it all, and if we don't understand, how can we possibly teach others about the eternal life that is found in Jesus Christ? We United Methodists don't believe in transubstantiation like our Roman Catholic friends, but have we made it clear to those who worship with us the great mystery of it all? Have we made it clear that Jesus is in fact the bread of life that nourishes us along this great journey? Have we made clear the promise that Jesus makes to us, in this bread and in this drink, that he will never leave us? After all, there may be more Janes out there looking for that person or congregation that can help them to better understand this great mystery of the Holy One of God.

September 1, 2024– Fifteenth Sunday after Pentecost

Song of Solomon 2:8-13; Psalm 45:1-2, 6-9; **James 1:17-27;** *Mark 7:1-8, 14-15, 21-23*

Jennifer Forrester

Preacher to Preacher Prayer

Gracious God, make us mindful of all the gifts we have received from above. Help us to be content and grateful, giving our love and lives to you all our days. Fill us with grateful hearts and help us to set aside anything that keeps us from welcoming your word and your love. Instill in us, again, your hope, your peace, your joy, and your love amid all that we encounter in this world, and remind us constantly, we pray. Amen.

Commentary

The world is ever changing. Everything in our lives can change in an instant, but what James is reminding us is that God is unchangeable and everything that comes from God is good. James is reminding us that every generous act and every perfect gift is indeed from above, but we also know that as it was then and even as it is now, there are many things of this world that become shadows, blocking the light. There are many things that cloud our perfect vision, but God's true word, the gospel, gives us all new life, taking away all of the shadows and clouds so we can see clearly the goodness of God once again.

James also gives us instruction on how to produce what is good. He writes: "Everyone should be quick to listen, slow to speak, and slow to grow angry" (v. 19). For it is behavior like this that will produce God's righteousness or good fruit, and that is our singular mission. I believe this is a great word for us today because all too often we speak and show anger first only to regret our words later. James reminds us of how we are to behave as disciples. We are to listen to one another before we speak. I am convinced that most divisive conversations could be avoided if we would adhere to these words from James. The way to righteousness for James was the joining of word and deed. It is being doers of the words. It is in the measure of one's hospitality to others that we are able to see God's will being done in this world. John Wesley himself focused a lot on the book of James writing: "But this cannot be done till we have given our hearts to God, and love our neighbor [and particularly those most in need] as ourselves."[1]

We live in a world that often does not love or follow God's ways. We live in a world where everyone is out for themselves. We worship and study the Scriptures, only to go out in the world and quickly conform to whatever surrounds us, forgetting what we look like the second we walk away from the mirror; forgetting who we are and whose we are. It is not enough to only be hearers, we must also put what we hear into practice. I believe this scripture reminds us as people of faith we are to not only quote scripture but to live it.

Bringing the Text to Life

It is hard work to live out all we learn from Jesus. I sometimes think it is even harder as the church. We know all that Jesus calls us to be and we even teach it, to love our neighbor, yet when faced with opportunity to live out the word as the church, we often fail. I often fail.

Recently, I attended a meeting at a nearby church. You know the kind—one of those meetings telling us how we are to conduct our next meeting. I walked in admiring the addition at the church where the meeting was held. It is a blessing that the church is doing so well, when so many churches are struggling today. It was beautiful. I noticed the architecture of the new entrance and how welcoming the color scheme was that they had chosen, and then there it was, plastered on every single door: "Restrooms NOT for Public Use." Suddenly the new space didn't feel so welcoming. I felt a little disappointed in the church, actually. Why not let those who might need to use the restroom come in? Aren't we, as a church, always complaining that people are not coming to church anymore? Maybe people don't feel welcome. But, I cannot be too hard on this particular church, because as I am sure you know, whenever we are judging how someone else has done something, we are often given our own opportunity to act, to be doers. Well, it was about three days later when the church I am serving discovered that someone experiencing homelessness was sleeping out in the church's garden under the pavilion where we hold worship on Sundays. The tug-of-war began. "Is it safe to let him stay there? Is he hurting anything? If we tell him he cannot stay there, are there other things we can offer him?"

Friends, we are often contaminated by this world. That contamination causes fear when we are confronted with those who are different from us. The world causes us to be fearful of the unknown. We are to remember who we are and be doers. We need to ask ourselves who is our neighbor?

September 8, 2024– Sixteenth Sunday after Pentecost

Isaiah 35:4-7a; *Psalm 125; James 2:1-10, (11-13), 14-17; Mark 7:24-37*

Jennifer Forrester

Preacher to Preacher Prayer

Gracious God, we know that you have all the power to help us in times of panic and fear, whether it be trouble, problem, pain, or sickness. We ask that you would cover us with your redeeming power according to your will. Strengthen those who are tired and weary, reminding them of the confidence and hope they can have in you, God. Amen.

Commentary

This text from the thirty-fifth chapter of Isaiah is part of a longer poem on the redemption of Zion in the period of time following the disaster of 586 BCE, when Edom took the place of Babylon as the enemy. The poem is reminding the people of hope and "is in fact an anthology of short prophecies of salvation, applicable to any situation in which hope breaks through the darkness of despair."[2] It was and continues to be the reminder that God can restore all things, and will.

The world was and is no longer what God meant for it to be. There is a difference between how things are, how we wish they were, and how they ought to be; often, that is frightening and painful, causing great uncertainty. There are many things that cause us this kind of fear and panic. Sometimes it is grief over the loss of a loved one, worries about our health or the health of others, and sometimes it is troubles at work, loneliness, or brokenness in our own families. The people were longing for their suffering to come to an end and that is still the case today. We long for a world where basic needs are met. We long for individuals, families, and nations to live in peace with one another. We have come to a place where we see the damage we have caused the earth and we long for it to be restored.

The beauty of the language of the poetic prophecy is written to bring new strength and courage. The terms and phrases used seem to make it more personal. For example, the phrases "your God" rather than "the Lord," and "divine retribution," that is, God's reward for being so steadfast in God's love for such wayward people, make the meaning of the text personal. The word *save*, as in salvation, is also used, which is not common in the earlier chapters of Isaiah. This is the reminder the people are given so they will know that God longs to be back in a right relationship with all of God's creation.

Bringing the Text to Life

We have all had our time of panic or fear. We may have even shared those stories with others; people who are close to us. As a pastor I have heard many stories of panic and fear from parishioners and friends, but I have also heard stories of the redeeming power of God that Isaiah describes in our text.

Recently a church member, and friend, shared her story. A story of God's divine intercession and how in the midst of the hardest time in her family's life, God showed up in a powerful way and saved her life. We won't get in to the politics of it in this commentary, but when in conversation with a friend of hers about the reversal of *Roe v. Wade* in June 2022, her friend made the comment that there is no way she could carry a child that she knew would die after birth. My friend said a lot struck her about the conversation, having lost a child that was ten days old herself, but she said what struck her the most was that her friend said her life would be over if she ever experienced child loss. In her reflection, she realized that her friend's comment was true.

My friend shared the story of the beautiful, but short, life of her daughter and what it was like to hold her lifeless body in her arms in a dimly lit NICU. She reflected on how her life suddenly became "a dichotomy of the 'before' and 'after' Ellie." She said she could barely recognize who she was anymore. And she lost more than their daughter and herself that day. She said, "There was so much loss." She lost friends. Some because they didn't know how to shoulder her burden and some because she wasn't able to be the friend she had once been to them. She said she had died that night with her daughter, but "what was born in the aftermath is something more beautiful than I could have ever imagined." My friend said she no longer took the little things for granted. She noticed things more than before. She danced in the rain with her other child. She loved more deeply and in her career, where she works with terminally ill people, she was better at her job because she was now equipped to carry burdens that others could not. She said even the love in her marriage was stronger because they "locked hands and fought for each other in ways we never had." She even experienced her faith in a way that changed her life. She saw God's love poured out through others and experienced the love and mercy of Jesus in worship.

Isaiah reminds us: "Be strong! Don't fear! . . . Here's your God . . . God will come to save you." Eyes will be opened, ears of the deaf cleared, the speechless will sing, the water will spring up in the desert (35:4-6).

September 15, 2024– Seventeenth Sunday after Pentecost

Proverbs 1:20-33; Isaiah 50:4-9a; Psalm 19; Psalm 116:1-9 or Wisdom of Solomon 7:26–8:1; **James 3:1-12***; Mark 8:27-38*

Beth LaRocca-Pitts

Preacher to Preacher Prayer

Most wise God, you are our teacher in every season. In the fall, when students return to school and teachers prepare themselves to share their knowledge, help us to teach one another of your goodness, your mercy, and your grace. Let us teach one another in humility, striving always to imitate Jesus Christ our lord, who taught us best through his love and sacrifice. Amen.

Commentary

The theme of speech, particularly the type of speech used to teach others, runs through two of the readings suggested for this Sunday. Isaiah 50:4-9a begins with the voice of God's Servant saying: "The LORD God gave me an educated tongue," to know how to respond to the weary with a word that will awaken them in the morning." This is a beautiful depiction of the quality of speech a teacher might employ to inspire and motivate others to learn. However, James 3:1 cautions that "not many of you should become teachers, because we know that we teachers will be judged more strictly." While this is not quite as poetic a depiction of the role of the educator, it nonetheless conveys how seriously the author of James takes the responsibility of those who would teach others. Only the mature may hope not to make mistakes when teaching, verse 2 states, implying that those who are young or new to the faith should be careful how they speak when they attempt to teach others.

The author then points out that though the tongue is a relatively small part of the body, as the organ of speech it has the same power to control and direct what happens to both the speaker and the hearer as a rudder has to direct a ship, or a bit to direct a horse. Like the tongue, the bit and the rudder are tiny when compared to an entire horse or a whole ship, yet they both control the direction that the larger entities of which they are a part travel. Speech, represented by the tongue, has the power to destroy by kindling the flame of discord and hate, and yet speech is also the medium by which we praise God. This causes the writer to urge their community to purify their speech, so that they may be consistent in using their tongues to bless and not curse, making sure their speech produces only good things and not evil. It should not be the case, James writes, that with one tongue "we both bless the Lord and Father and curse human beings made in God's likeness" (James 3:9).

Bringing the Text to Life

The power of words to hurt or to heal has never been more clear than it is in our current age of social media and the twenty-four-hour news cycle. From hucksters who sell worthless cures to desperate people, to cruel voices that tip fragile teens over the edge toward suicide, our society seems to have abandoned any attempt to rein in the myriad of carelessly destructive voices that pervade social media. It is as James proclaims in 3:8, "No one can tame the tongue, though. It is a restless evil, full of deadly poison." It is a well-known fact that conspiracy theorists are now flooding the airwaves and cyberspace with outlandish fabrications every day with no thought to the anguish and havoc this causes in the lives of those swept up in their lies. In one notable case, the brother and the parents of Seth Rich, a staffer with the Democratic National Committee, who was shot and killed in what the police believe was a botched robbery, had to sue several individuals as well as Fox News to end years of distress caused by the network's amplification of conspiracy theories claiming that their son was murdered by the people he worked with, turning him into something he never was, namely, the victim of a left-wing assassination and coverup. Eventually Rich's family won an apology from those concerned, but they had to fight for that apology for years.[3]

Similarly, the families of the Sandy Hook shooting victims had to repeatedly sue Alex Jones of Infowars over his continued insistence that the whole incident was staged to defame the gun industry. Parents had to confront Jones in court and force him to admit he was lying when he claimed their dead children never existed, that their violent deaths never happened. Jones magnified the incredible pain endured by these parents at the loss of their children by unleashing his scores of listeners who then harassed and hounded them based on Jones's outrageous lie.[4] It is rare that those who spread such lies are ever made to account for the damage their lies have done. Once spoken, a deliberate and targeted lie can ruin lives and cause untold disruption. One could argue that the prevalence of such high-profile cases has made Americans more aware of destructive speech, and thus may somehow bring an end to such speech in our culture. But if it takes such excruciating battles in court to make potential offenders think twice about their lies, one has to wonder if, still, the price of truth is too high.

September 22, 2024– Eighteenth Sunday after Pentecost

Proverbs 31:10-31; *Wisdom of Solomon 1:16–2:1, 12-22; Jeremiah 11:18-20; Psalm 1; Psalm 54; James 3:13–4:3, 7-8a; Mark 9:30-37*

Beth LaRocca-Pitts

Preacher to Preacher Prayer

Our God, you have created each one of us with unique personalities and gifts and competencies. You have given each of us strength. You have given each of us insight. Help us to recognize and value the strength and skills, not only of ourselves, but of others, so that all your children may serve you to the full extent of their power. Amen.

Commentary

On first glance, Proverbs 31:10-31 seems to reinforce some unfortunate and outdated stereotypes about women and their sphere of influence, appearing to limit the life and work of women to the confines of the family home. In addition to this, older translations of verse 10 imply that "capable" or "virtuous" women are rare, such that one could conclude that the majority of women are not capable or virtuous. In the King James Version verse 10 reads: "Who can find a virtuous woman?" The RSV reads, "A capable wife who can find?" The CEB translation is better, "A competent wife, how does one find her?" But there is even more nuance in the opening line that describes this woman. The Hebrew phrase translated "a virtuous woman," or "a capable woman," really should be understood to be a description of a woman at the height of her powers, the ideal woman. If the word *man* were substituted for the word *woman* in this passage, a good English translation of the phrase would be "warrior" or "strong man," an image that calls to mind a man at the height of his strength and power. So what makes the woman described here the epitome of female power? First of all, we should think of her less as a "housewife," and more as a frontier wife, or a wife whose household is also a family business. She is her husband's partner in their economic life as much as in their domestic life. In verses 13 through 15, we see her manufacturing textiles out of wool and flax, trading her products for imported food, running a household staff, and supplying them with whatever they need.

Unlike the false stereotype of women as chattel in the Old Testament, this woman has control of enough money to buy land and establish a vineyard in addition to her other business as a weaver and cloth maker. She is industrious. She generates income for the family. She gives to the needy out of her abundance. She provides for her household so that all are well fed, well cared for, and unafraid for the future. She is wise and kind, beloved and respected by her family. Finally, in a wonderful indictment of our modern tendency to favor superficial qualities like physical beauty over character, verse 30 states, "Charm is deceptive and beauty fleeting, but a woman who fears the LORD is to be praised."

One final word of praise for the woman of Proverbs 31:10-31 is seen in the structure of the passage. These twenty-two verses form an acrostic poem, one in which each verse begins with a letter of the Hebrew alphabet in order until all twenty-two letters are used. Acrostic poems are thought to symbolize perfection, completion, or wholeness, such that this poem describes the perfect, complete, and whole image of the ideal woman. And just as the book of Proverbs begins with the image of God's wisdom (in Greek, *Sophia*) personified as a woman, the woman of Proverbs 31:27, is said to be "vigilant [in Hebrew, *Tsofiah*] over the activities of her household." In this way the poet likens the woman being described here as a reflection of the Wisdom that is a part of God.

Bringing the Text to Life

So often we look at others and project onto them what we think they are like based on their appearance or their situation. Looking at the women of the Bible we can project onto them our presumptions about what their lives were like without reading the text plainly for what it says about them. We presume they were subjugated by an overwhelming patriarchy, so we don't see their power or their victories even when they are clearly described for us in the text. Many times in life we presume we know who people are and what people are capable of doing when, in fact, we can know nothing about them if we don't take the time to truly see them.

Most people who passed Oseola McCarty on the streets of Hattiesburg, Mississippi, wouldn't have had any idea what she did for a living or whether or not she was wealthy. Those who did know her knew that she worked taking in washing, but even they might have been surprised to learn that after she was diagnosed with cancer in her nineties she gave her life savings of $150,000 to the University of Southern Mississippi for a scholarship so that young people trying to go to college wouldn't have to work as hard as she did.[5]

When people watched movie siren Hedy Lamarr on the silver screen of the 1930s, most saw only her mesmerizing beauty and had no idea that she was an accomplished self-taught scientist and inventor, who would eventually go on during World War II to patent an invention that could help prevent signal jamming used against radio-guided torpedoes. Modern Wi-Fi, GPS, and Bluetooth are partially based on the process Lamarr patented.[6] People are more than their outward appearances and impressions we get from the contexts in which they live. We deprive ourselves of meeting extraordinary people if we summarily decide we have nothing to learn from them.

September 29, 2024– Nineteenth Sunday after Pentecost

Esther 7:1-6, 9-10; 9:20-22; Numbers 11:4-6, 10-16, 24-29; Psalm 124; Psalm 19:7-14; James 5:13-20; **Mark 9:38-50**

Beth LaRocca-Pitts

Preacher to Preacher Prayer

There are more ways to worship you, most holy God, than there are stars in the heavens or sand on the seashore. Help us to appreciate the beautiful diversity of your children and to appreciate all the many ways your creation praises you. Make us advocates for one another and help us to see how our greatest differences can become our greatest strengths. Amen.

Commentary

It is common to picture the growth and development of diversity within Christian communities as a tree rising from the ground and branching off into new expressions of the faith through time. It is an apt image in many ways, but it is also incomplete if we do not also draw the picture with a cross-section showing the numerous and twisted roots branching off and stretching out underground. There never was one original Christianity that splintered into numerous expressions after having once been united. There were always many expressions of belief in Jesus Christ that proliferated from the very beginnings of the faith, and were then pared down through the councils and condemnations of the patristic period, producing what we think of today as the proto-orthodox faith.

Mark 9:38-50 gives evidence of this early diversity, citing one example from the time of Christ's own life. The disciples see someone who considers Jesus's name a word of power and is using it to do exorcisms. The disciples seem to resent this man. They do not know him and presumably he does not know Jesus, and yet he is using Jesus's name, essentially, as a magic word. They tell Jesus that they tried to stop him, but his reaction was no doubt surprising to the disciples because Jesus does not appear to be troubled by this man. He tells the disciples that "no one who does powerful acts in my name can quickly turn around and curse me. Whoever isn't against us is for us" (v. 39). He goes on to teach his disciples to be careful how they treat others whose faith is not the same as theirs. He compares others who might be hurt by careless or haughty treatment to children who can be discouraged and disedified by the condescension of those more mature than they are, and be led to sin because of it. Those who would hurt another in this way would be better off dead, says Jesus. No one should have such hubris about their own faith that they would willingly destabilize the faith of another, less mature believer.

Finally, Jesus points out to his disciples that no one is actually so rigid in their beliefs about sin that they would take extreme action, such as amputation, to rid their own lives of it. The early church also must have decided that this was hyperbole on the Lord's part in that eye gouging and limb severance did not become sacramental practices in the church. In closing, Jesus compares his followers to salt, which has specific purposes based on its specific qualities. If those qualities are lost the salt is worthless. So Jesus advises the disciples to be true to themselves, to be authentically who they are, and allow others to be authentically who they are and in so doing they will be able to live peacefully with those who are different from them.

Bringing the Text to Life

How we respond to those who are different from us, and yet proclaim to share a Christian identity with us, is a challenge that faces modern Christians every day. No one can anger us or aggravate us more than those who claim to be a part of our faith tradition but whose actions or beliefs are abhorrent to us. On an essential level, we do not want to be thought to be "like them." It can be annoying, for instance, when traveling to Israel, to realize that secular Israelis often think that all Christian people believe the same things. It can take some convincing to get the point across that not all practicing Christians are conservative. Not all Christian clergy are men. Not all Christians abstain from alcohol. Describing someone, like a Quaker for example, as an evangelical leftist seems as oxymoronic to the Israeli ear as describing an ultraorthodox rabbi as someone who enjoys eating bacon. It doesn't make sense. Our need to set ourselves apart from one another on the basis of specific doctrine makes us appear like a family that tries to disown some of its members.

The United Methodist Church is currently in the midst of this sort of mutual disowning, with two sides each trying to stake a claim for authentic Wesleyanism while simultaneously ruling the other side out of bounds. It often seems to be a matter of branding. One side does not want to be a part of a denomination whose "brand" includes affirmation of same-sex marriage or affirmation of God's call to ministry on the lives of gay people. The other side does not want to be part of a denomination whose "brand" does not affirm these things. Sadly, there does not seem to be a middle ground whereby both sides can each hold such disparate beliefs and yet still be willing to claim kin with the other. For this reason, the tree that is the Christian faith looks certain to branch yet again in the near future. If the gospel contained in Mark 9:38-50 speaks anything into this reality, it may be that Jesus would advise us to let one another be, to bless one another to go our separate ways. We should understand what the "saltiness" is that makes each of us who we are. We should claim that giftedness for ourselves and learn to live into it such that we can part from one another in peace. We may not be able to love the same people and affirm the same people in the name of Christ, but if we can love those whom God sends to each of us, hopefully, at the end of all things, more love will be shared.

October 6, 2024–Twentieth Sunday after Pentecost

Job 1:1; 2:1-10; **Psalm 8**; Hebrews 1:1-4; 2:5-12; Mark 10:2-16

Will Zant

Preacher to Preacher Prayer

Glorious God, how majestic is your name throughout the earth. As I open your holy Word,
inspire awe in me at your creation and at the task of proclamation. Amen.

Commentary

One of the central themes of this passage is that the glory of God brings revival to the soul. This theme of glory is expressed in three ways.

First, this psalm from King David speaks to the overwhelming glory we experience in God's creation. You can almost see King David staring into the night sky: "When I look up at your skies, at what your fingers made—the moon and the stars that you set firmly in place" (Psalm 8:3). When we look at a work of art, typically we are drawn to want to know more about the artist. Who were they? What was their life like? What inspired their painting? The same can be said about God. When David looks at the moon and stars, he is drawn deeper into the mystery and majesty of God. We can imagine the weary nature of King David's reign. From his many wars (2 Samuel 8:14) to the tragic death of his son Absalom (2 Samuel 18:33), perhaps gazing at the stars and heavens above provided him a needed moment of transcendence.

It is a humbling experience to wonder how God makes room and time for us. Most people have looked at a night sky and questioned how God could remember them and their circumstances. Preachers can help give voice to such worry and wonder. After David has admired the stars and heavens, he then expresses his humility:

What are human beings
that you think about them;
what are human beings
that you pay attention to them? (Psalm 8:4)

Perhaps David is thinking about God's own mercy toward him when he committed adultery with Bathsheba (2 Samuel 11:1-27). God cared enough for him to pay attention to his need for forgiveness. More broadly, David's question helps us consider the grace of God toward us and our need for divine intervention.

Second, God's glory is expressed in human activity through our care of God's handiwork. While forgiveness belongs solely to the mercy of God, David also acknowledges that humans can play other important roles in caring for God's people. David answers the question by acknowledging that God's glory continues to shine through the deployment of our gifts to care for others and creation:

> You've made them only slightly less than divine,
>   crowning them with glory and grandeur.
> You've let them rule over your handiwork. (Psalm 8:5-6)

Humans are part of God's providential plan to care for the needs of his people. We are the answer to David's question, "What are human beings that you pay attention to them?"

And last, Jesus is the ultimate manifestation of God's glory. As we bring this exploration of glory forward to the New Testament, we are reminded that the same glory of the heavens above is found in Jesus:

> The Word became flesh
>   and made his home among us.
> We have seen his glory,
>   glory like that of a father's only son,
>   full of grace and truth. (John 1:14)

God's glory is alive in the flesh through Jesus. There is nothing more glorious than to experience Jesus alive in our life. As people experienced Jesus's signs throughout John's Gospel, they too were filled with the same awe that David had as he looked at the heavens above. Through his turning water into wine, his raising of Lazarus from the dead, and Jesus's own death and resurrection, Jesus has revealed God's glory and brought revival to the world.

Bringing the Text to Life

In many liturgical traditions, this Sunday is also World Communion Sunday. Therefore, this Sunday can lend itself to celebrating David's words of praise: "how majestic is your name throughout the earth!" (Psalm 8:1). Preachers can share their experiences of witnessing natural landscapes across the world as a reflection of God's glory. However, praising creation requires caution. King David addresses the psalm to the Lord and not creation itself. King David is sure to exalt the majesty of God's name.

In applying this scripture, preachers can also address the importance of spending time in God's creation. In a world that is becoming increasingly sedentary, star gazing can provide children and adults a healthy appreciation and awe of God. This scripture pairs well with Vincent van Gogh's famous painting *Starry Night*. In his art, Van Gogh turned deeply painful experiences into expressions of comfort and consolation, which he found in nature. Van Gogh confessed to "having a terrible need of—shall I say—religion. Then I got out at night to paint the stars."[1] In one of his letters to his brother Theo in 1888, he wrote, "The sight of stars makes me dream." Van Gogh was a devoted Christian and his love for nature expressed in his paintings resembled David's own musings.

This scripture provides a poignant opportunity to show people how much they matter to God. Most people have wondered how God could care about them and their needs in the midst of such a vast creation. How do our lives matter in the grand scheme of things? The astonishing part about our Christian claim is that Jesus never forgets us. He knows us by name. He told parables about a shepherd who was willing to leave ninety-nine sheep behind in search of the lost one.

Lastly, this scripture helps us encourage people to use their gifts as an act of divine care for God's people and creation. Each person in the pews has wondered how their gifts and talents impact the order of the universe. Our job as preachers is to help these people connect the dots and see how their gifts are part of God's providential plan. You might include the apostle Paul's listing of spiritual gifts from 1 Corinthians 12:28 as a starting point to encourage congregants. When we lean into our God-given talents to comfort others, it's just as glorious as the heavens above.

October 13, 2024– Twenty-First Sunday after Pentecost

Job 23:1-9, 16-17; Psalm 22:1-15; Amos 5:6-7, 10-15; Psalm 90:12-17; Hebrews 4:12-16; **Mark 10:17-31**

Will Zant

Preacher to Preacher Prayer

Gracious God, open my ears to your holy word. Give me the words to help realign your people's hearts with their true treasure, which can only be found in you. Amen.

Commentary

In Mark 10:17 we learn that eternal life is not something to be obtained. This man's problem is clear from the outset. He views life in terms of possessions. His ease of purchasing has fooled him into believing that salvation can be earned. In the preceding passage (10:13-16), Jesus makes clear that the kingdom of God is a gift to be received like a child would and not something to be possessed.

Each person has their unique sins and vices that prevent them from following Jesus more closely. Jesus does not call everyone to leave behind their possessions. Jesus recognizes that this man's love for his possessions has become demonic. How could he expect to follow Jesus when he has such a collection of treasures to consume his time? Possessions are ultimately what bind his life.

In Mark 10:21-22 Jesus recognizes the critical moment of either transformation or rejection. Mark tells us that Jesus looked at him carefully and loved him. Jesus takes this moment seriously because he knows he is about to deliver words that will challenge this man's worldview. Jesus's motives spring from his love for this man and not from judgment. Jesus is seeking to realign his life with the good news of the Kingdom. In preaching this scripture, the tone of the message is equally as important as the message itself. This message is an offering of a life-change through repentance.

The treasures in heaven mentioned in verse 10:21 are not just about a future reality. These treasures are not about delayed gratification or about future heavenly mansions. One can experience the treasures of God on earth. In fact, Jesus clarifies to the disciples that these heavenly treasures are available now. Anyone who makes a sacrifice to follow Jesus "will receive one hundred times as much now in this life" (Mark 10:30).

To exchange his earthly treasure for heavenly ones is a gift to be received today. When preaching this text, it is important to remind people that the gifts of a new life in God can be received today and not just after death. Preachers can point congregants to the fruit of the spirit (Galatians 5:22-23) as an example of these new heavenly treasures. Another scriptural reference is John 3:16 in which Jesus promises Nicodemus eternal life during this life. Eternity begins now. Charles Wesley's famous hymn, "Love Divine, All Loves Excelling," also picks up on this theology: "Come, Almighty, to deliver, let us all thy life receive." When one follows Jesus, they receive the very indwelling presence of God during this life.

In Mark 10:27 we learn that all things are possible for God. Having heard Jesus describe the difficulties for rich people entering the Kingdom, the disciples feel discouraged and overwhelmed. In fact, the disciples are shocked and ask, "Then who can be saved?" (v. 26). Their response gives voice to the reactions and questions many of your congregants will be asking about such a claim from Jesus. The preacher has an opportunity to accent and relate to their shock. A preacher can help name the deceiving rationales we give to our constant need for accumulating possessions. However, Jesus encourages them with a message of hope. God can liberate them from all forms of slavery, including the debilitating grip sin has over their lives. Jesus reminds them all things are possible, even overcoming the forces and lures of wealth. The gospel has always been about the transforming power of God to work in our lives and save us from our sin.

Bringing the Text to Life

On the one hand, preachers do not need to shy away from addressing people's demonic relationship with possessions. On the other hand, preachers are wise to approach this sensitive topic with grace and empathy. Congregants are searching for authoritative spiritual guidance on how they can best relate to money and use it well. Each day they receive different and opposing messages about wealth. It is important to note that Jesus is not condemning wealth altogether, but instead its grip over one's life. In many churches, pastors launch their annual stewardship campaign around this time of year. It will feel disingenuous to preach a text like this and make a connection to giving financially to the church. Perhaps a better approach on this particular Sunday during stewardship is to preach on how God can help us develop a spiritually healthy relationship with money and possessions.

Lastly, Jesus studied this man carefully because he understood the theological weight in the moment. His future hung in the balance. While delivering this message, preachers might pray for their own motives. Study the people's faces in the pews on this day. If delivered out of deep love for congregants, this moment can radically change a person's life and help them realign their hearts to God's kingdom way of life. In offering illustrations, consider showing this man not as he is, but as he could be, had he chosen to follow.

While it is certainly appropriate to share stories of missionaries who sold all of their possessions to follow Jesus into the mission field, you might also consider less dramatic ones that might better relate to your listeners. Is there a story of a father who sold his boat and gave the proceeds to the youth mission trip because he was spending too much time away from his high schooler? People are searching and longing to know that a life transformation is possible. By the authority of Jesus, you get to proclaim that all things are.

October 20, 2024–
Twenty-Second Sunday after
Pentecost

*Job 38:1-7, (34-41); Isaiah 53:4-12; Psalm 104:1-9, 24, 35c;
Psalm 91:9-16; Hebrews 5:1-10;* **Mark 10:35-45**

Will Zant

Preacher to Preacher Prayer

*Gracious God, as I open the Scriptures today, remind me that we are servants of your Holy
Word. Help us not to use the task of preaching for our own glory. Instead, take our time
and toil to give life and liberation to your people. Amen.*

Commentary

Jesus's glory is defined by the cross and not by worldly power. Having witnessed
Jesus's transfiguration on the mountaintop a chapter earlier, James and John realize
Jesus is more than a teacher. They have witnessed his glory. Perhaps they believe
they have an inside track to a privileged seat at Jesus's right and left hand. They can
imagine the power and glory of such status. It is clear from the outset that these
two brothers do not fully understand Jesus's mission. Take note of their request.
"Teacher, we want you to do for us whatever we ask" (10:35). It is almost comical.
Parents can relate to children asking them to say yes without knowledge of their
request.

Jesus is leading the disciples on his journey to the cross, but they are unsure of
what the cross means. Throughout Mark's Gospel, the cross is the defining image. It
is a symbol of suffering that reveals God's glory. Jesus's glory is defined by the cross.
When preaching this passage, pastors should help redefine glory. God's glory is not
about gaining leverage or power over other people. It is not a privileged place at the
high seat of a table. Glory is revealed through humble service and even a willingness
to suffer for the mission of God. We can certainly sympathize with James and John.
They did not have the vantage point of knowing the whole story. Their reaction is

– 121

meant to reveal the human temptation to be drawn toward glory for ourselves instead of God's glory that is meant to liberate.

This encounter with Jesus also speaks to clergy. We too are tempted to confuse personal glory for God's glory. Our preaching is not a vessel for self-glorification. Our task is to have Jesus use us to liberate God's people from their sin.

Jesus calls his followers to a different way of life. Upon learning the requests of James and John, the other disciples get angry. The jockeying for power has officially begun among the disciples. Jesus takes this moment to reframe how they understand power. He tells them not to follow the example of the Gentiles. There is no spiritual ladder to climb for one's own self-aggrandizement. Instead, they are to live differently. "But that's not the way it will be with you. Whoever wants to be great among you will be your servant" (Mark 10:43). Jesus followers are to reveal the heart of God by their service to others. Servant leadership is a hallmark of Christian discipleship. It is better to serve than to be served.

Preachers must be careful in speaking about servanthood. Preaching the ministry of servant leadership should not inadvertently promote taking advantage of others and their willingness to serve. History is rife with examples of such abuse. This needs to be noted. Taken seriously, Jesus's teachings on servanthood are life-altering. Serving the needs of the poor, helping pick up the chairs after Wednesday night dinner, or visiting the lonely neighbor across the street become the way of the cross that leads us to the glory of the Resurrection and personal transformation.

Jesus came to liberate us from sin. Jesus is beginning to reveal the purpose of the cross. He will "give his life to liberate many people" (Mark 10:45). Notice that Jesus uses the verb "give." He will give his life. It will not be taken. His giving of his life is his way of loving and liberating us. The gospel is about God doing for us what the Law could not do. Only Jesus and his death on the cross could save us from this human condition. It is my hope that preachers will feel encouraged in their preaching by this affirmation from Jesus. In service to Christ, preachers give their time and toil into the weekly sermon. In God's mysterious way, the Holy Spirit liberates the listeners in our pews.

Bringing the Text to Life

There's a well-traveled story about a minister lamenting to his spouse. "Honey, there just doesn't seem to be many great preachers. I feel like there are no pulpiteers left in the church. If you were to guess, how many great preachers do you think are left in our conference?" His spouse responded, "One less than you think."

As ministers, we too, like James and John, can confuse our human hunger for personal glory with our divine calling of sharing God's glory. God's glory is defined by the cruciform way of living called the cross. The glory of the Resurrection can only take place if there is a cross. As we set out to begin our wondrous and awesome task of preaching, we are reminded that Jesus came "to give his life to liberate many people." Our preaching should do the same.

This text falls in ordinary time during the fall. In the rhythm of many churches, the fall is a season of service opportunities. Congregants are offered opportunities to serve on church mission projects and in areas like children's ministry. Jesus's teaching on servant leadership is a wonderful opportunity to connect the dots for congregants seeking to grow in their discipleship. Discipleship is marked by the cross and its cruciform way of life. The glory of the cross will help congregants experience the glory of the Resurrection.

October 27, 2024– Twenty-Third Sunday after Pentecost

*Job 42:1-6, 10-17; **Jeremiah 31:7-9**; Psalm 34:1-8, (19-22); Psalm 126; Hebrews 7:23-28; Mark 10:46-52*

Will Zant

Preacher to Preacher Prayer

Gracious God, fill my life with joy. Remind me that your mercy is greater than our offenses. May the words I prepare on your behalf restore your people to the abundant and good life. Amen.

Commentary

God's people can trust Jeremiah's words of hope because of his courage in delivering the words of despair. Jeremiah calls the people to sing joyfully because God has saved his people (Jeremiah 31:7). Out of context, these words might come across as benign words of encouragement to a group of people experiencing a hard time. The context of this joyful poem is everything. Jeremiah calls forth praise in the midst of the people's pain.

This passage is a beacon of hope in a book filled with doom and despair. The book of Jeremiah captures the experience of the Babylonian Exile from 587 BCE. While most of Jeremiah's prophetic work is filled with warnings to the people of Israel about God's impending judgments, Jeremiah also turns them toward a future of hope. His words of hope are believable because he has also told them the truth about their sin. This dual theme of proclaiming despair and hope is first articulated in God's calling of Jeremiah:

> "This very day I appoint you over nations and empires,
> to dig up and pull down,
> to destroy and demolish,
> to build and plant." (Jeremiah 1:10)

Notice that four out of the six verbs are about destruction. Preachers can sympathize with Jeremiah's difficult tasks (imagine preaching four out of six sermons on destruction). But preachers can also relate to the need to help their members face the truth about the hard and ugly parts of life. When we walk our congregations through the hard journey of exile we can emphatically sing joyfully with them as we witness God's redemption in their lives. They can indeed "sing joyfully" for the Lord has saved the people of God. Jeremiah's words are in rhythm with the New Testament theme of cross and resurrection. The triumph of the Resurrection is heard most impactfully when it is set within the context of the cross.

A second theme is about the healing power of gathering after a devastating event.

I'm going to bring them back from the north;
    I will gather them from the ends of the earth. (Jeremiah 31:8)

Jeremiah is speaking to the remnant of people left during the horrors of the Babylonian Exile. Some Israelites are still in Jerusalem while others have been scattered throughout the land of their captors. In the midst of a disastrous event, one of the powerful sources of healing is gathering together. For these exiled Jews, God desires to bring them back to the temple, which was the heartbeat of the Jewish faith. Pastors might think of the joy and healing their congregations experienced when gathering together for the first time amid the COVID-19 pandemic.

Lastly, God provides the assurance of his love and care, which is what the people needed most.

I will lead them by quiet streams
    and on smooth paths so they don't stumble.
I will be Israel's father,
    Ephraim will be my oldest child. (Jeremiah 31:9)

Jeremiah comforts the people with the knowledge that God will guide them like a shepherd guides sheep by quiet streams. You can hear the pastoral imagery of Psalm 23. The experience of the exile incited feelings of abandonment, displacement, and disorientation. God is reorienting the people to his care and love. The imagery then turns to God as a father and is likened to the love a parent has for a child. The people will again flourish under God's gracious providence. When preaching this passage, your words can take the shape of a guiding shepherd who is leading the people back to familiar pastures after hard times in their lives. The job of the preacher this day is to evoke praise and joy over God's mighty deliverance of his people, even if that joy is expressed in tears.

Bringing the Text to Life

As you prepare your sermon, consider how you can invite the congregation on the journey from devastation to hope, sadness to joy, sin to redemption. Each congregant is looking for directions to that path. Your sermon is also an opportunity to deal with the unpleasant parts of people's lives. Addressing such matters is necessary for them to feel understood and less alone. Preaching can portray the devastating parts of life as long as you lead them out of that experience to the promise of resurrection. When you arrive at joy, show that joy in its fullness and depth. Jeremiah encourages the people to sing joyfully and raise their voices.

Jeremiah reminds us that preaching prophetically has the dual task of proclaiming the cross and resurrection. On the one hand, pastors must be willing to address the sin and despair of the cross or else the preaching can feel out of touch with real life. One might think about Ernest Hemingway's famous quote on writing: "If it is all beautiful you can't believe in it. Things aren't that way."[2] On the other hand, prophetic preaching leads the hearer to good news. There is the temptation to think of prophetic preaching as simply telling the hard truth. Prophetic voices today must never leave the people in despair. Jeremiah proves that prophets can preach good news too!

An illustration could focus on a figure like Archbishop Desmond Tutu. One of the most endearing parts about Tutu's witness was his unique ability to tell the unvarnished truth about the evils of apartheid in South Africa while simultaneously making room for forgiveness and reconciliation. We need both. More locally, this text provides a great opportunity to celebrate the testimony of a congregation member who has found joy and redemption after years of spiritual exile. Whatever examples you choose, may you and your congregation celebrate with tears of joy.

November 3, 2024– All Saints Sunday, Twenty-Fourth Sunday after Pentecost

Isaiah 25:6-9; Revelation 21:1-6a; **John 11:32-44**

Paul Christy

Preacher to Preacher Prayer

Oh Lord, on this special All Saints Sunday and this special week as we remember those who have gone on before us, we pray that you will inspire us with the memories and the stories, but most of all inspire us in your word. May we listen to the way you speak to us this day, and as we listen may we hear the word you would have us preach, teach, and speak this week. Open our hearts and our souls and our minds to receive your grace and to proclaim your grace. Amen.

Commentary

This is such a familiar text that many times I am convinced we all hear the beginning of the story and then we shut down because we know the rest of it. We know that Jesus raises Lazarus from the dead. Yet, if we pay attention, the text is filled with images of not only the gospel, but of the ministry of Jesus. We need to remember that Jesus must have been good friends with Mary, Martha, and Lazarus because anytime Jesus was near their home, he seemed to stop in to eat and visit. But if we read the whole story we see that Jesus waited four days before "rushing" to see Lazarus. In verse 32, Mary says; "Lord, if you had been here, my brother wouldn't have died" (John 11:32). Mary knew Jesus was special and knew he could do anything, even heal the sick, but Lazarus was beyond sick now. He was dead. You see, as pastors we often hear of a death or a surgery and we drop everything and go running to be with these families, often neglecting our own families. I remember many times being away and cutting a vacation short to go be with families during times of need. However, Jesus waits. There may be a lesson for all of us who care for others. Yet, while I can see how some could make this a story about pastoral care at its basic level, it is a story about resurrection and life.

If this is a story about seeing and believing and the power and the glory of God, then I love the exchange of Martha and Jesus. Jesus asks where they have laid him and they go to the graveyard and Martha says, "Lord, the smell will be awful! He's been dead four days" (John 11:39). I love the King James Version of that verse: "Jesus said, Take ye away the stone. Martha, the sister of him that was dead, saith unto him, Lord, by this time he stinketh: for he hath been dead four days" (John 11:39 KJV). Yet, in verse 40 we read, "Jesus replied, 'Didn't I tell you that if you believe, you will see God's glory?'" (John 11:40). Gerard Sloyan in his commentary on John through the Interpretations Series says this: "The purpose of the miraculous restoration to life is not that the family should be reunited in happiness, much as Jesus would have reveled in that family joy. It is that Martha should 'see the glory of God' (v. 40) once she had believed and that many of the Ioudaioi would likewise believe in Jesus (v. 45)."[2] On this day we celebrate as All Saints Day, we believe in the glory of God because we believe that our loved ones are with God. That is reason to celebrate in the midst of loss and sadness. When a loved one dies, we know that is not the end of the story. Isn't it great to celebrate the lives of those who have gone before us?

Bringing the Text to Life

I happen to have the blessing or the curse of being from a family of United Methodist pastors. Now when I say that I really mean that. There are fourteen ordained deacons or elders in my immediate family. We all felt the call to ministry in different ways, but the point is that is a lot of preachers in one family. I give you this non-important fact to tell that I heard my older sister preach the Lazarus story many years ago, and she focused on the fact that when Lazarus comes out of the tomb, he is bound up with burial cloth. Then Jesus said, "Unbind him, and let him go" (v. 44b NRSVUE). Now, looking at the text from the CEB, the meaning changes just a little when it is translated "Untie him and let him go" (v. 44b).

The point is well taken using that image because there are many things that bind and tie us up in this life. We can be bound by addiction. We can be bound by grief. We can be tied up with hatred and an unforgiving heart, and we can be tied up with (fill in the blank).

I like to hear the story of Lazarus and understand that there is nothing that can bind or tie me up so much that God's love and grace can't set me free. If Jesus can raise Lazarus from the dead, just imagine what Jesus can do for you? What is binding you? What is tying up your people? What is binding your church?

November 10, 2024– Twenty-Fifth Sunday after Pentecost

Ruth 3:1-5; 4:13-17; *1 Kings 17:8-16; Hebrews 9:24-28; Mark 12:38-44*

Paul Christy

Preacher to Preacher Prayer

Gracious God, you give us life and purpose. As I study your word this day, I pray that you speak to me your words of truth and that you speak through me your words of truth. May your Scriptures be brought to new life in my prayer and study and may you teach me so that I can speak your grace and be in your presence. May I let the meditations of my heart give voice to your love. Amen.

Commentary

I am not going to lie to you. This text is riddled with issues that are still happening today, many of which we wish not to talk about with our church people. Did Naomi really tell her daughter-in-law to trick Boaz into marrying her? Did Ruth do what her mother-in-law asked her to do without any regard for herself? Why is this first part of chapter 3 included in the story of Ruth? These are all good questions as we begin to reflect on the story of Ruth, but this day we focus on the beginning of chapter 3 and the end of chapter 4.

Now, as a preacher and teacher, I am good with the way the scripture ends because that is where we come to understand the significance of the book of Ruth. Ruth will play a pivotal role in the Jewish and Christian faith. Boaz and Ruth have a son named Obed, and Obed has a son by the name of Jesse, and Jesse has a son by the name of David, the great king of Israel, and Jesus is from the lineage of David. So, Ruth is an important and pivotal book in all the Scriptures. I am amazed at how God uses unlikely people to spread God's love and grace. Yet, we still have to get through chapter 3, don't we?

For me, chapter 3 is important to the story because up until this point Naomi is still in full-blown grief over all the tragedy in her life; her husband and two sons had died suddenly. She had to leave to come back home and it really was a tragedy, but Ruth was the one who showed and taught her hope. In chapter 3, this is the first time we see Naomi not worried about herself but about Ruth. Naomi says to Ruth, "My daughter, shouldn't I seek security for you, so that things might go well for you?" (Ruth 3:1). Notice here that Naomi does not refer to her as her daughter-in-law but instead her daughter. For me that is significant. Naomi begins the healing process because she is thinking of others before herself. Naomi wants Ruth to get dressed up and feel good about herself so that Boaz will notice her and know her as a true servant. Ruth is a servant because she never puts her needs in front of anyone else's. She served Naomi and she went with Naomi to Judah, a foreign land to her, all the time thinking of Naomi and not wanting her mother-in-law to be alone. Now we see a turn for Naomi. She is getting the gentle message of what it means to be a servant. She is thinking of Ruth instead of herself.

The preacher and teacher will do well to talk about what it means to be a servant and how we are taught throughout the Scriptures to have a servant's heart. I believe Ruth is the picture of the word *servant*.

Bringing the Text to Life

I had a roommate in college who became a banker. After we graduated, he worked his way up to be the city executive for his bank and was what all of us would call successful. Then he called me up one day and said that he was feeling called to ministry. I said, "No you're not! You're a banker!" He replied, "Paul, I want to talk to your dad about being a pastor. Do you think he will talk to me about that?" I assured him that he would and my dad called up and told me that he wanted to take me and my friend golfing.

We got to the course and my old roommate was asking my dad what it took to be a pastor and Dad said very little, but let me tell you what my dad did do. He picked my old roommate's ball out of the cup on every putt he hit. Dad handed him his club every time. When my roommate laid his wedge on the green while he putted, Dad was there to pick it up and hand it to him. Every good shot he hit my dad would say, "Now that was a good shot and I am proud of you for hitting it so well."

Finally, on hole eighteen, my friend, frustrated that Dad wasn't filling his head with what it took to be a pastor, said "John, for eighteen holes I have asked all kinds of questions about ministry and what it takes to be in ministry and you haven't said a whole lot. Tell me how can I be successful in ministry!" My dad said, "Here's your ball. I picked it up out of the hole so you wouldn't have to bend down." Then it hit my friend. "John, so you are saying being in ministry is about serving and helping others?" Dad just smiled and said, "Dennis, that's what it means to be a disciple of Jesus Christ, to serve others before yourself."

For me, Ruth is that model of a servant and how God can use us all to be an example of a servant!

November 17, 2024– Twenty-Sixth Sunday after Pentecost

1 Samuel 1:4-20; Daniel 12:1-3; **Hebrews 10:11-14, (15-18), 19-25;**
Mark 13:1-8

Paul Christy

Preacher to Preacher Prayer

Gracious God, as we study your word this week, oh how we desire you to give us fresh insight, to come to a deeper understanding, and to grow in your grace. May your grace surround us so that even in our weakest moments, we may feel your strength. When we doubt, remind us that this is just a growing edge. So now, dear Lord, may you speak to us that we may live your word in grace-filled and loving ways. Amen.

Commentary

I need to confess something right away: I am not really a huge fan of the Letter to the Hebrews. Part of the reason is because I had a professor at Duke many years ago who was not a huge fan of it, and I guess his influence on me colored my opinion of the letter. However, after being in ministry for over thirty-three years, I have come to appreciate the images and the power of the language contained in this important letter. It is amazing at times the influence our words can have on others, isn't it? When we come to understand that the Letter to the Hebrews was written to Christians who were heavily influenced by the Jewish faith and Jewish customs, then it makes a little more sense. The writer is trying to help the reader understand the power and the grace of the life and ministry, death and resurrection of Jesus Christ.

Take our scripture this week from this letter. The images of a priest making sacrifices for sins is to remind the early Christians that because of Jesus there is no need for sacrifices because Christ made the perfect sacrifice. "Every priest stands every day serving and offering the same sacrifices over and over, sacrifices that can never take away sins. But when this priest offered one sacrifice for the sins for all time, he sat down at the right side of God" (Hebrews 10:11-12). The writer goes on to remind the reader, and yes, even us today, that "we have confidence that we can enter the holy of holies by means of Jesus' blood, through a new and living way that he opened up for us through the curtain, which is his body, and we have a great high priest over God's house" (Hebrews 10:19-21).

If we ever wonder why we gather in worship as a church, the writer of Hebrews gives us an answer. We gather to not only worship God, but we gather to proclaim Jesus Christ and the atoning sacrifice Christ made for the world. We do not need to pray a certain way, give a certain way, be a certain way to gain God's grace or acceptance. We have been given the gift of life through Jesus Christ. So, what I have come to discover is that the Letter to the Hebrews is not just for first- century Jewish Christians but also for modern-day disciples of Jesus Christ. It is always a good reminder to preach Christ, and how Christ died for our sins. We do not earn nor are we good enough or rich enough to gain forgiveness. We receive it through Jesus Christ.

Bringing the Text to Life

As a young man, I was a camp director for a United Methodist camp in the mountains of Western North Carolina. One day we had an evangelist drop by the camp during the middle of the season while kids were running all around and we had a lot going on that day. But this evangelist was a family friend and his name was Wallace Chappel. He and my dad were the best of friends. Dr. Chappel stopped me right outside the dining hall at Camp Carolwood and after seeing all the activity that was happening, he said "Paul, can we pray?" I said absolutely, and offered for us to go into my office. He said, "Paul we will pray right here and he grabbed my hands and kids were laughing and talking all around us and Dr. Chappel began to pray. As he prayed, the kids stopped laughing and talking and before I knew it the circle that began with just the two of us had grown to about thirty people. He prayed a powerful prayer and in that prayer he said, "Lord let us never be ashamed of the gospel, never ashamed."

His prayer left an impression on me because there are times when I do not want to make anyone feel awkward or uncomfortable in my ministry. But then I think back to Wallace Chappel not being ashamed to pray Christ right outside the dining hall of Camp Carolwood. As the church, as disciples of Jesus Christ, we are to proclaim Christ! And let us never be ashamed.

November 24, 2024– Twenty-Seventh Sunday after Pentecost

2 Samuel 23:1-7; Psalm 132:1-12, (13-18); Daniel 7:9-10, 13-14; Psalm 93; Revelation 1:4b-8; **John 18:33-37**

Ron Bartlow

Preacher to Preacher Prayer

Lord, we start this day contemplating what it means to call you such. Even in the midst and conflict of many competing claims on us, it is the desire of our hearts to confess you as ultimate. Consecrate our intent, bless our service, and help us celebrate "thy kingdom come." Amen.

Commentary

At the end of November in an election year it is probably more appealing (and definitely safer!) to preach on gratitude and thanksgiving than to plan and commemorate the liturgical Sunday of "Reign of Christ," formerly known as "Christ the King Sunday." This liturgical moment marks an intersection of religion and politics, faith and power, spirituality and ideology. Many of the day's lections echo this intersection, evoking images of kings and power, thrones and crowds. We find Jesus there at the corner, a Jewish prisoner standing before a Roman governor.

In the full encounter between Jesus and Pilate (18:28–19:16), the CEB includes the word *king* nine times, with two additional references to "kingdom" in this pericope (18:36) and one to the far-off "emperor" later (19:12). In modern political systems, we may forget the depth of what such descriptions of sovereignty entailed.

This must be an important encounter, as it is one of those rare moments that is detailed in all four of the Gospels, with Pilate's question asked each time (cf. Matthew 27:11; Mark 15:2; Luke 23:3). Perhaps this moment is so pregnant with meaning that it is even open to multivalent interpretation: Are Pilate's many questions disguised assertions, or earnest inquiries? Do we read in his demeanor certainty, or curiosity? If we imagine Pilate authoritative, we might see an antagonist; if instead we imagine Pilate curious, we might see a fellow seeker.

However we read Pilate's questions, let us not miss that in the pericope Jesus never directly claims for himself the title of which Pilate asks. "You say that I am a king" Jesus says (v. 37), redirecting the discussion of kingly power to his assertion that he "came into the world . . . to testify to the truth." Rather than evoke throngs over which he might hold and exercise power—say, the power of a governor over a person's life or death!—Jesus declares "everyone who belongs to the truth listens to My voice" (BSB), reminiscent of earlier comparisons in John to sheep and shepherds.

If Jesus is a "king," and if we celebrate the "reign of Christ," then what we mean by these otherwise worldly political concepts must change. The connection Jesus creates as our Lord or sovereign is not the hierarchical power of far-off emperors and governors holding dominion over life and death; it is instead a new connection not of this world, what many call the new kin-dom in Christ. Christ was born to bring truth to those who might listen, truth we may spend the entirety of our time under his rule seeking, learning, and embodying. We are united not through obligation or obedience to a dominating political power, but through baptism and welcome into a grace-filled, life-giving, and life-affirming connection.

Distracted by the power dynamics of his day, Pilate misses his chance at learning from Christ's truth. He returns to balancing the power of his office with the threat of rebellion, to satisfying the Jewish rulers' and people's desires while maintaining Roman peace and order. One may wonder if, had Pilate's desire to hear and listen to the voice of truth before him been greater, the world of politics and power as we know them might have changed. One might also wonder if, standing before Jesus in Pilate's place, we might have been able to set aside the expectations of the world around us and say, "I want to be one who listens."

Bringing the Text to Life

The images that we carry might inform and inspire those to whom we are called to preach. What are the images or thoughts that come to your mind when you think of kings and kingdoms? Do you imagine fairy-tale kingdoms of adventure, or oppressive regimes of history? Is your inclination to think of short-lived, tumultuous rulers like Nero or long-lived, servant monarchs like Queen Elizabeth II?

Does your community have a particular relationship with power and politics? Preaching on Christ's reign might sound different at a crossroads near Pennsylvania Avenue compared with a corner in the cornfields of Iowa.

Jesus, standing before Pilate, evokes to me an image of one standing at peace, silent, speaking truth, listening. This image of Jesus inspires me to confidently pray, "thy kingdom come on Earth as it is in heaven." Such a prayer reminds me to remain steadfast and faithful to the shepherd who has faithfully led me into this kingdom.

November 28, 2024– Thanksgiving Day

Joel 2:21-27; Psalm 126; 1 Timothy 2:1-7; **Matthew 6:25-33**

Charley Reeb

Preacher to Preacher Prayer

Lord, forgive us when we forget that you are enough. Save us from the endless and anxious pursuit of more and grant us the peace that passes all understanding—the peace that only you can provide. Lord, take our fear and replace it with gratitude for all the ways you care for us. Teach us to remember your faithfulness to us so that we may live with joy and thanksgiving. Amen.

Commentary

The Sermon on the Mount contains many challenging lessons and the selected text for Thanksgiving is certainly one of them. "Don't worry," Jesus commands. He tells us to observe nature and notice how lilies and birds go about their business with Zen-like ease. Be more like that, Jesus says. Well, easy for him to say, right? He's the Son of God! But we humans are often at the mercy of our overactive brains that have been wired by God to worry for self-preservation. Besides, in our world, there is a great deal to be worried about!

Over the years, preachers have been quick to point out that Jesus was not commanding that we live reckless lives without healthy concerns. The word Jesus used for worry means to "worry anxiously." Some preachers have used this insight as an opportunity to share with their congregation that a certain amount of worry and fear is healthy and can actually be productive. One classic example of such a preacher was the great pulpiteer J. Wallace Hamilton who preached the often-quoted and "borrowed" sermon "Make a Friend of Your Fear!" In the sermon, Hamilton states, "Like a pain in the body, fear in the soul is a distress signal warning of some inner wrongness, a healthy prod to do something constructive to correct that wrongness."[2] It is hard to argue with that insight. Hamilton goes on to explain that worry and fear have a rightful place in our lives but, like anything else

God has created, worry can run amok and paralyze us. This is that kind of worry Jesus is telling us to avoid.

But how do we avoid being paralyzed by worry? This is the question that our listeners will be desperately asking. I believe the text suggests three ways we can prevent worry from taking over our lives and stealing our peace. We could do worse than preparing a sermon around these three ideas.

First, we put worry in its rightful place by remembering how God provides. The constant refrain in this passage is the way God provides that which is needed for even the seemingly insignificant things of the earth (birds, lilies, grass). If God takes care of the lilies of the field, we can certainly count on God to deliver when we are in need. And God has done so, again and again! I believe this is why this text is chosen for Thanksgiving Day. As we look at our bountiful table of food on Thanksgiving, how "much more" (v. 30) God provides for us will be evident and should naturally lead to a prayer of thanksgiving. Remembering God's faithfulness has the ability to calm our fears.

Second, Jesus's soft admonition in verse 25 is helpful: "Isn't life more than food and the body more than clothes?" I imagine if many of us took an inventory of the things we worry about, much of it would be trivial in the grand scheme of life. It is unfortunate that so much of what we spend our precious energy worrying about is inconsequential. Think of what we could accomplish by putting our time and energy into more useful pursuits (cue the next paragraph!).

Third, when we make serving God our number one concern, our worries have a way of losing power over us. Jesus puts it this way: "desire first and foremost God's kingdom and God's righteousness, and all these things will be given to you as well" (v. 33). If we spend each day dedicated to pursuing the things of God, we won't have time to worry about those matters that take energy from us. In fact, we will find that many of our concerns dissipate or work themselves out.

The passage in Matthew is a clear reminder that God can be trusted. This sets us free to serve God with joy and thanksgiving.

Bringing the Text to Life

J. Arthur Rank, an English executive, chose to do a rather clever thing to get a handle on his worries. He chose to worry only one day of the week—Wednesday. Whenever he started to worry about something, he would write it down, put it in his "worry box" and forget about it until the following Wednesday. Interestingly, whenever Wednesday came around, most of the things in his worry box that troubled him the week before were already settled. It would have been a waste of time to worry about them.[3]

The lesson in Rank's story is simple: *Fix what we can control; give God what we can't control.* Most of us worry about things we have no control over. Most of us also worry about things we could easily solve. The problem is that we often spend too much time, energy, and resources on those things we can't control instead of those things we can control.

"Instead, desire first and foremost God's kingdom and God's righteousness, and all these things will be given to you as well. Therefore, stop worrying about tomorrow, because tomorrow will worry about itself. Each day has enough trouble of its own" (vv. 33-34).

December 1, 2024–First Sunday of Advent

Jeremiah 33:14-16; Psalm 25:1-10; 1 Thessalonians 3:9-13;
Luke 21:25-36

Jim Somerville

Preacher to Preacher Prayer

Christ, here you come again! And while we love you and celebrate your coming, it always seems to take a lot of work to get ready for it. So, give us the strength we need to make it through, and beyond that, fill us with the kind of joyful anticipation our parishioners often feel in this season. Because it's not just anyone who's coming; it's you!

Commentary

Let's begin with a definition. In general, the word *advent* refers to "the arrival of a notable person, thing or event,"[1] but through the years Christians have used that word to refer to the coming or *second* coming of Christ. Did you catch that? It's not only the first coming we talk about in Advent, not only the long-ago birth of the baby Jesus, but also his second coming "in power and great glory," and traditionally we talk about that on this first Sunday. And can I tell you this? Nobody likes it. When someone steps up to the pulpit and reads the Gospel lesson about "people fainting with fear and foreboding of what is coming upon the world," church members start squirming in their pews. They may not say it out loud but they're thinking, "Aren't we trying to get ready for Christmas? Why do we have to talk about people 'fainting with fear and foreboding of what is coming upon the world'? Christmas is supposed to be a happy time!" Yes. Yes, it is. And Christmas *is* a happy time. It is the celebration of the birth of the baby Jesus. It is the culmination of the Advent season. But it is not the inauguration of the Advent season. For centuries now the church has used this First Sunday to talk about Christ's second coming, and nobody likes it.

So, I have a suggestion.

What if, instead of *beginning* the Christian year with all this talk about Christ's second coming, we simply tacked it on to the *end* of the Christian year? That way you could have "Reign of Christ" Sunday, as we did last week, and then follow it with "Return of Christ" Sunday this week, and then the Christian year would start all over again with a three-week season of Advent that was completely devoted to getting ready for the first coming of Christ at Christmas. How about that?

I don't know who's in charge of the Christian year or who gets to make changes to the calendar but I do know this: whether it happens on the First Sunday of Advent or the last Sunday of the Christian year, we need at least one Sunday devoted to the doctrine of the Second Coming. If you don't believe it, then maybe we need to take a look at the history of the church and the witness of scripture.

Bringing the Text to Life

From the very beginning, the followers of Jesus have heard that the Christ who was crucified, buried, and on the third day rose from the dead will someday come again. In today's Gospel lesson Jesus says that after all these terrible things happen, and after the power of the heavens are shaken, "then they will see the Son of Man coming in a cloud with power and great glory. Now when these things begin to take place," he continues, "straighten up and raise your heads, because your redemption is drawing near" (vv. 27-28 ESV). Those disciples who were there at his ascension heard the angels say, "Men of Galilee, why do you stand looking into heaven? This Jesus, who has been taken up from you into heaven, will come in the same way as you saw him go into heaven" (Acts 1:11). Years later, the Apostle Paul promised that when the time is ripe "the Lord himself will descend from heaven with a cry of command, with the voice of an archangel, and with the sound of the trumpet of God" (1 Thessalonians 4:16). It hasn't happened yet, but that doesn't mean it won't.

Church historian Bill Leonard remembers considering that idea when he was fifteen years old. He said that he lay awake in his bunk at church camp praying that Jesus would *not* return. Earlier that night, at worship, the camp pastor had said that he might. He warned all those boys and girls at camp that they needed to be ready. "Jesus could come before morning!" he thundered. But Bill Leonard prayed that he wouldn't. He was fifteen years old! He was just waking up to the mysteries and wonders of the opposite sex. There was one particular girl he hoped to sit beside during Bible study the next day. "Please, Jesus," he prayed. "Don't come back tonight. Wait a little longer. Please?"

Apparently, his prayer was answered.

That's how it is when things are good: the news of Christ's second coming starts to sound like bad news, like the rude interruption of a perfectly wonderful life. We'd just as soon he stay put. But what if things weren't so good? What if life were difficult, and desperate, and grim as they were when this Gospel was written, what then? Would the cataclysmic events of today's Gospel lesson begin to sound like good news? Would we begin to lean forward in our pews and say, "Yes, preacher! Tell me more about that!"?

Maybe today we could begin to see that hope for the good news that it is, and maybe, along with the early church, we could begin to sing, "Come, thou long expected Jesus, born to set thy people free; from our fears and sins release us, let us find our rest in thee."

That's something to hope for, isn't it? Remember this: *when you are in a place where things can't get any worse, they are about to get better.* May you never find yourself in such a place, but if you should (as many of Jesus's disciples actually did), just bow your head and pray, "Come, Lord Jesus." You will be in good company. The followers of Jesus have been praying that prayer for nearly two thousand years, and one of these days, in a way we can only imagine, that prayer will be answered.

December 8, 2024–Second Sunday of Advent

Baruch 5:1-9 or Malachi 3:1-4; Luke 1:68-79; Philippians 1:3-11;
Luke 3:1-6

Jim Somerville

Preacher to Preacher Prayer

Why, Lord? Why do we have to spend two weeks with John the Baptist on our way to Christmas? We are ready for Christ to come now! Or are we? Maybe it takes more than we think to prepare the way of the Lord. Maybe there's more work to be done in us than we want to admit. Help us get ready, Lord—your way—for we pray in your name. Amen.

Commentary

One December evening one of my Jewish friends asked, "Are you waiting for Advent at your church?" "Well, no," I said. "We're not waiting for Advent; we're waiting for Jesus!" But when I thought about it later, I realized he was right.

But so was I.

The word *advent* means "coming," so when he asked, "Are you waiting for Advent?" he might have said, "Are you waiting for the Coming?" Well, yes, we are, but it's not just any coming we're waiting for: it's the coming of Jesus, and it's not just his first coming; it's also his second. But last week it dawned on me that in Advent we wait and prepare for the One "who is and who was and who is to come," as it says in the Book of Revelation (1:8 NIV). So we look forward to his coming in the future, we celebrate his coming in the past, but we also get ourselves ready to meet him in the present.

Our Gospel reading for this Sunday focuses on John the Baptist, and when he told people to get ready for the One who was to come. He wasn't talking about the second coming of Christ, and he wasn't talking about the birth of a little baby. John was talking about the One God had chosen to make things right in the world—the Anointed One, the Messiah—and he talked as if he might come at any moment.

Why does Luke spend so much time telling us about John the Baptist? Because in some ways John is as important to the story of salvation as Jesus is. In this week's reading from the Hebrew Bible the prophet writes, "Behold, I send my messenger, and he will prepare the way before me. And the Lord whom you seek will suddenly come to his temple" (Malachi 3:1 ESV). The Jews of Jesus's time believed that before the Messiah came there would be this other person, this Messenger, who would prepare his way. It was an integral part of their messianic expectation. And so Luke takes his time telling John's story, assuring us that this is the one God has sent to prepare the way of the Lord.

Bringing the Text to Life

John began to preach in "the fifteenth year of the reign of Tiberius Caesar," Luke tells us, and then he makes reference to all the other people who were ruling at that time in various places, drawing lines across the map and circling dates on the calendar, until he has established with pinpoint accuracy the precise moment when the word of God came to John in the wilderness.

And I've been wondering what that word was.

- It might have been the word *finally*, because it had been four hundred years since there had been a prophet in the land. All that talk about returning from exile, rebuilding the temple, and restoring Israel to its former glory had pretty much been forgotten. Now Israel was just one more province in the vast Roman Empire, and hardly the most important one.

- Or it could have been the word *now*, because after all those centuries of silence *now*, again, God was speaking to his people, and speaking to them through one who looked and sounded very much like one of the prophets of old, who came to them "in the spirit and power of Elijah" (Luke 1:17), as the angel had said.

- But I think it was the word *repent* because this is how John finally decided to "make ready for the Lord a people prepared"—by preaching a baptism of repentance for the forgiveness of sins, by convincing people that they needed to turn their lives around and get themselves cleaned up before they met the Lord. And John didn't mean that they would meet him someday when they died; he meant here, now, any minute. He meant that he might look up from his baptizing one day and see "the Lamb of God who takes away the sin of the world" (v. 29).

Maybe you've seen that Norman Rockwell painting *The Homecoming*, where the soldier comes home unexpectedly and catches his family by surprise. It is a happy surprise, but a surprise all the same. You can see his mother, leaning out over that porch railing to welcome him with open arms. But can you imagine if she had known he was coming? She wouldn't have been wearing her apron and that ratty old cardigan sweater. She wouldn't have been caught making bread, with a dusting of flour still on her face and her hands. She would have been wearing her Sunday best, as would her husband and all of her other children. That house would have been sparkling from top to bottom. The table would be set with her best crystal and china, with the smell of a pot roast in the oven coming from the kitchen.

That's what John was doing when he preached a baptism of repentance for the forgiveness of sins. He was giving people a chance to get ready for the one who was coming, and he was coming any minute! They didn't have any time to delay. It would be like that soldier calling his mother from the train station and telling her he would be home in ten minutes. She would hang up the phone and look at the mess and spring into action. And that's what I mean when I talk about getting ourselves ready to meet Jesus in the present, because he is not only the one who is to come, in the future, and not only the one who was, in the past, a baby in Bethlehem, he is the one who is, even now, Emmanuel—God with us.

December 15, 2024–Third Sunday of Advent

Zephaniah 3:14-20; Isaiah 12:2-6; **Philippians 4:4-7***; Luke 3:7-18*

Jim Somerville

Preacher to Preacher Prayer

Lord we are so close to Christmas we can almost taste the joy. But joy is elusive. It's like a fist full of jelly. The more we squeeze it the more it slips through our fingers. So, spoon feed us, Lord. Fill us with joy. For the sake of the people we serve, and for our own sakes. Amen.

Commentary

This is the Third Sunday of Advent when we often focus on the theme of joy. But here's the problem: we can talk about joy, we can sing about joy, but we can't make ourselves joyful. While we can do the things that give us pleasure and pursue those things that make us happy, joy is a different matter. It comes to us, and it often comes to us when we least expect it. So how can Paul say, in Philippians 4:4: "Be glad in the Lord always! Again I say, be glad!" (or *rejoice*)? How can he command us to have an experience over which we have no control?

Well, he can't, of course. It doesn't make any sense. But he, being Paul, does it anyway and it might help us to consider the source of his joy. Paul writes these words from prison. He is uncertain of his future and—for the moment at least—unable to fulfill his mission. And yet he commands the Philippians to rejoice in the Lord always. "Again I will say it," he insists. "Rejoice!" (NIV). Why? It's right there at the end of verse 5: "The Lord is near."

Barbara Brown Taylor seems to understand. In an article called "Surprised by Joy" she says, "The only condition for joy is the presence of God. Joy happens when God is present and people know it, which means that it can erupt in a depressed economy, in the middle of a war, [or] in an intensive care waiting room."[2]

It happened for Paul while he was in prison, writing to those Philippians. He sensed that the Lord was near and it gave him goose bumps of joy. It may explain why we read this passage from Luke's Gospel on this Third Sunday of Advent, a passage in which John the Baptist seems to be preaching nothing but bad news. "You children of snakes! Who warned you to escape from the angry judgment that is coming soon? Produce fruit that shows you have changed your hearts and lives. And don't even think about saying to yourselves, Abraham is our father. I tell you that God is able to raise up Abraham's children from these stones. The ax is already at the root of the trees. Therefore, every tree that doesn't produce good fruit will be chopped down and tossed into the fire" (Luke 3:7-9). That doesn't sound very joyful, does it? But people were coming to hear him and they were asking what they should do. They sensed that the Lord was near, and it gave them goose bumps.

Bringing the Text to Life

What should they do? John told them that they should get ready for the Lord's arrival in the most practical ways imaginable, and when they wondered if he might be the Messiah he said: "I baptize you with water, but the one who is more powerful than me is coming. I'm not worthy to loosen the strap of his sandals. He will baptize you with the Holy Spirit and fire. The shovel he uses to sift the wheat from the husks is in his hands. He will clean out his threshing area and bring the wheat into his barn. But he will burn the husks with a fire that can't be put out" (Luke 3:16-17). Luke ends his account by saying that with these and many other exhortations John proclaimed "good news to the people" (3:18).

You have to wonder: "a fire that can't be put out"? How is that good news? Only because the one who is more powerful than John is coming—Christ himself is coming. Or, as Paul might put it, "The Lord is near." You can hear his footsteps in the hall. And when he comes he will bring justice to the earth. He will take what is wrong and make it right.

Can you see how that sort of thing might give Paul goose bumps, especially if he were locked up in some smelly prison cell? "Rejoice," he said to the Philippians. "Rejoice! The Lord is near." It may have been for him a prayer for deliverance as much as anything, but for us it can be something else altogether.

- When two or three of us gather together in his name, the Lord is near.
- When we laugh out loud in a Sunday school class, the Lord is near.
- When we discover some new truth in the Bible, the Lord is near.
- When the Holy Spirit moves and swirls among us, the Lord is near.
- When we sense his presence as we gather for worship, the Lord is near.

So rejoice, Paul says, like someone who knows that joy can come to us every time Christ comes near to us. And he comes to us all the time—in all sorts of ways—and every time it is joy, pure joy.

He is that word—*joy*—made flesh.

December 22, 2024–Fourth Sunday of Advent

Micah 5:2-5a; Luke 1:46b-55; Hebrews 10:5-10; **Luke 1:39-45, (46-55)**

Jason Micheli

Preacher to Preacher Prayer

O King born in Bethlehem, the House of Bread, as we look and long for your second coming to our broken and war-torn world come once again this Sunday in the ordinary creatures of word and water and wine and bread. Be our shepherd whose voice we recognize and obey; so that, we might proclaim to sinners the promise that the Lord has done and is doing and will do great things for us. Amen.

Commentary

According to custom, Mary would have been no older than sixteen when she became engaged. According to tradition, Joseph most likely was an older man, marrying for the second time. According to Torah, because Mary and Joseph were betrothed, any sexual activity prior to her wedding day would have been understood as adultery not fornication (Deuteronomy 22:23).

What if a woman in Mary's position claimed she had been raped? What if her husband had brought false charges against her? What if she flatly denied any wrongdoing? For such murky, disputed circumstances, Numbers 5 prescribes the "water of bitterness" wherein a suspected adulteress would be brought before a priest, required to let down her hair, and under oath drink a mixture of ash, holy water, and the ink from the priest's written indictment. The woman's oath, "May the LORD make you a curse and a harmful pledge among your people, when the LORD induces a miscarriage and your womb discharges" (v. 21b). If guilty, according to Numbers 5, the woman would become sick. If she did not become sick (an unlikely happening) she was acquitted.

Whatever we may think today of such customs, this was the reality that governed Mary's world. It was the reality in which she nonetheless, hearing Gabriel's news, replies, "May it be with me according to your word" (Luke 1:38 ESV).

Mary would have known the likelihood she'd be accused of adultery. Just as surely she would have known the proscribed punishment she might receive. Mary would've known how Torah insisted Joseph divorce her, and she certainly would've known that whatever child she gave birth to before marriage, regardless of the angel's promises, forever would be regarded as an illegitimate child and banned from the cultural and religious life of Israel. Still, in the face of all those likelihoods, Mary summons the courage to say, "May it be with me according to your word."

The obvious conclusion we can draw from this scene is that Mary had a faith sufficient to say yes to the vocation God had for her. We can assume Mary had faith that the God of Israel is merciful and would protect her. We can assume Mary knew from her scripture stories of women—suspect women—who nonetheless played a part in God's plan and were safeguarded and ultimately rewarded by God. Mary must have known, we can imagine, that God's call is very often a summons to serve and to suffer for love's sake.

When Mary assents to the Annunciation, she does so knowing her life will never be the same. Her Nazareth, she had to have known, would never look at her the same way again. It's in Mary's yes to God here in Luke 1 that we can spot for the first time the shadow of her Son's cross. If we allow Christmas to be merely about sentimentality, we miss how Mary suffers for the Messiah before the Messiah himself suffers. Indeed, one could speculate that Jesus learns suffering love and the demands of faithfulness on his mother's knee.

Bringing the Text to Life

Marie worked with me in the after-school program at Princeton Junior School when I was in seminary. Marie was the school librarian. She and her family were refugees from Liberia. Marie had a rich, East African accent and singsong-y, soulful voice. She always spoke incredibly slowly, as if she wanted to linger over every happy syllable that life gave her. And she had a laugh that began somewhere deep in her belly and always ended with her embracing in her arms whoever was nearest to her. If you didn't know her or her story, you might notice that Marie's hands looked rougher than the hands of someone who handled books for a living. You might notice that her arms were taut and looked like they'd been exercised by clenching them in prayer, or by scraping out a life or by pointing with ferocity. She was a big woman but perhaps a better way of putting it was that Marie was a solid, immovable woman.

Soon after the dictator Charles Taylor violently wrested control of her country, Marie and her family became hunted. She and her husband had been civil servants, just ordinary people, neither wealthy nor well known. They were just ordinary people who worked five days a week and on the weekends taught Sunday school at their Methodist church. When a modern-day Herod imposed his power over them, Marie's faith in a different Kingdom compelled her to act. She and her husband began advocating and agitating for the poor who had so suddenly been swept to the margins of the government's concern.

They harbored and hid away those who'd been labeled outcasts and enemies by the new regime. They refused to accommodate no matter what it might mean. At first, it meant harassment and then threats that went from veiled to overt. Finally, attempts were made on their lives. They never relented. She didn't talk about it much and certainly not with any bravado. I only learned her story in snippets told over time. Once, when the after-school students were having a snack of animal crackers and apple slices, I asked her if she and her husband had been "political." I asked if that's what had prompted and prepared them to resist. Marie just let out a delicious laugh and said, "That's what your government called us, political refugees." She bit the head off of a lion animal cracker and added, "But no, we weren't political. We were just Christians."

"Were you ever afraid?" I asked her.

She looked at me over the rim of her glasses, clearly wondering how I could be in seminary and still ask such a question. "Oh, I suppose," she said, "but what we were doing was too important." And then in the same voice she always had when she read to the children, the tone of voice that let you know the moral of the story was coming, she said, "Besides, if what you're doing is what God is doing, then what is there to be afraid of?"

In Roman Catholic tradition, Mary is most often depicted as nice and perfect. In our Christmas crèches, she's gentle and passive. She's sweet and fresh-faced on Hallmark cards, and in Christian art for two thousand years she has been somber, sober, soft, and white-faced. But if the gospel stories are true, then I think a simple 4" x 6" snapshot of Marie would get closer to the real Mary than anything da Vinci or Caravaggio painted. Because more so than Michelangelo, Marie would've known and understood that Jesus is born with monsters at his manger and that Mary delivers him into the world at a cost to herself we seldom pause to dwell upon. That Mary does so is an uncomfortable reminder that we need not be Christ in order to be Christians. We too can stand in the kingdoms of this world and gesture to an alternative that arrives through Mary's belly.

December 24, 2024– Nativity of the Lord

Isaiah 9:2-7; Psalm 96; **Titus 2:11-14***; Luke 2:1-14, (15-20)*

Jason Micheli

Preacher to Preacher Prayer

Lord Jesus, you are my righteousness, I am your sin. You took on you what was mine, yet set on me what was yours. You became what you were not, that I might become what I was not. Make my words to be what they are not apart from you; so that, the Word that was made flesh in Mary's belly might come again veiled in my ordinary words. Amen.

Commentary

Before Jesus Christ is your example, he is your gift. The Apostle Paul orders how we are to understand Christ in his letter to Titus: "For the grace of God has appeared, bringing salvation to all . . . [through] Jesus Christ who gave himself for us to redeem us from all lawlessness and to purify for himself a people for his own possession [Gift] who are zealous for good works [Example]" (2:11-14 ESV).

First, Christ is your Gift, and only after is he your example. About tonight's "beautiful text," the Protestant Reformer, Martin Luther, says, "If these fires do not stir you, you are colder than cold"[3] because the promise is that we have *everything* through him. Everything that ultimately matters we already have through him who has been gifted to us. This is the promise delivered tonight to the shepherds. We have righteousness, Christ's own. Jesus's permanent perfect record according to God's law is laid over top of us at baptism like an irremovable suit of forgiveness. We have justification. That is, in the Lamb's Book of Life, next to your name it does not read "Not Guilty." It reads "Totally Innocent." And there's nothing you do that can undo it. We have everything through him. We have salvation. He saved us, Paul writes. It's accomplished. Salvation is received not achieved. Everything has already been done. He has set you free from death and given you eternal life not as your wage—something you earn—but as your inheritance—something gifted to you by another. We have everything through him who has been gifted to us.

It's laying ahold of this gift that changes us according to Christ's example. This is what Paul means in verse 12 that the gift of God's grace trains us to live holy lives in the present age. The reason you must take Christ as your *gift* before you take him as your *example* is that the gift, the gospel, is how God changes you—from the inside out—to live into Christ's example.

Gift, example.

When it comes to understanding the gospel, these two words—*gift* and *example*—are the most important words and precisely in that order, because when you reverse the order (*example, gift*) you are left with no gospel at all. The example of Christ would be in vain if Christ were not first a gift, because no one can truly follow the example of the one born tonight unless they are born again by the gift of God's grace. As Paul explains the importance of this ordering in his Letter to the Romans, the Law—the example—is powerless to produce what it prescribes and, thus, it only accuses us. Only the gospel, the gift of God's grace for you, can create in you what the Law commands. Only the promise that everything has been done for you has the power to get you to go and do.

Gift, example.

This is why we do not call him Saint Jesus. No, the message the angels declare is, "For unto you is born this day in the City of David a Savior, who is Christ the Lord" (Luke 2:11 ESV). Five hundred years ago, as he worked on translating the New Testament into German so that the Scriptures would be accessible to ordinary people, Martin Luther wrote a brief preface titled, "A Brief Instruction on What to Look for and Expect in the Gospels." In it Luther writes, "Be sure, moreover, that you do not make Christ into a Moses, as if Christ did nothing more than teach and provide examples as the other saints do, as if the Gospel were simply a textbook of teachings or laws. . . . The chief article and foundation of the gospel is that before you take Christ as an example, you accept and recognize him as a gift, as a present that God has given you and that is your own. This means that when you see or hear of Christ doing or suffering something, you do not doubt that Christ himself, with his deeds and suffering, belongs to you. On this you may depend as surely as if you had done it yourself; indeed as if you were Christ himself."[4]

Before Jesus Christ is your example, he is your gift. And for all those wearied by this world, that's good news. It's good news, because when Jesus is your gift before he's your example, it takes earning out of the equation. There's nothing you have to do to deserve the gift because it's already been given to you.

Bringing the Text to Life

During the pandemic shutdown, I hunkered down and watched two classic, quality television programs (maybe you've heard of them) called the *The Bachelor* and *The Bachelorette*—all twenty-four and sixteen seasons, respectively. If you're aware of this shameless and tacky dating show, then you know that every episode concludes with the rose ceremony wherein the bachelor or bachelorette gifts a rose to the girl or guy they believe earned it. The gift protects the recipient from elimination.

What makes *The Bachelor* and *The Bachelorette* such guilty pleasures is how contrived and inauthentic the dates are. The prospective mates are all performing because they're trying to earn the rose and not be eliminated. They're trying to measure up to the bachelor's or bachelorette's ideals and therefore they are not free.

Example, gift.

However, once in a while, the rose ceremony comes at the very beginning of the show. For example, in season fifteen of *The Bachelorette*, Hannah gave her rose to Cameron—I mean, Cam—before the season even began. And so Cam entered the relationship knowing there was no chance he would be rejected, no fear he would be eliminated, no threat he would be sent home. And if you watch the dates where the rose has come at the beginning—where the gift has preceded any earning—they're normal. The two are at ease with each other. They're free to laugh and cry, and they begin to open up and reveal their true selves.

"For unto us a child is born."

Unto *you*.

God gives you the gift up front, right at the beginning of the story. And God gives you the rose that is Christ himself again and again, including tonight, in his Word, in Water and in Wine and Bread, which remind you that by your baptism into his suffering, death, and resurrection, you were irrevocably removed from the naughty list. You've got the rose already. You don't need to impress the Bridegroom. You'll never be sent home. So no matter what life has dealt you, you're free to be. You can live your life in the grace of God, you can live your life, at least for moments, at ease, in the peace of God, which surpasses all understanding, without fear, and in perfect love. This is God's promise to you tonight in this baby. *For unto us a child is born.*

December 29, 2024–First Sunday after Christmas Day

1 Samuel 2:18-20, 26; Psalm 148; **Colossians 3:12-17**; Luke 2:41-52

Jason Micheli

Preacher to Preacher Prayer

Lord Christ, just as your Holy Spirit has clothed us with the gift of your righteousness so now clothe yourself in the meager, ill-fitting words of your preachers so that your people might discover the boldness to follow you where they otherwise would fumble and fail. Amen.

Commentary

The Apostle Paul wrote to the Colossians roughly a generation *after* Jesus and 250 years *before* the Gospel *about* Jesus converted the empire. When Paul wrote to the Colossians, following Christ made you like an unwelcome immigrant in a hostile land. For the Christians in Colossae, you couldn't accept Jesus as Lord without rejecting Caesar as Lord. To make a commitment to Christ was to make enemies. So, you didn't join a church without thinking about it. Seriously and hard. In fact, the church wouldn't let you. The church first required you to undergo rigorous catechesis, throughout the long season of Lent. Then, and only then, would you be led outside the sanctuary on Easter Eve to a pool of water. There the church would strip you naked. And facing the darkness you would renounce Caesar and Satan and all their works. Then, like Pharaoh's soldiers, you would be nearly drowned in the water three times and, rising up from the water as Jesus from the grave, you would turn the opposite direction to affirm his Lordship and every practical implication that now had for your life. I certainly wouldn't want to strip naked, plunge down into night-cold water, and then stand around with a crowd of church people looking at me and what God gave me. To do something like that, you'd really have to feel and believe that Jesus Christ is Lord.

And yet—those same Christians who faced down Caesar and spit in sin's face and renounced the world and took the plunge into a new one, naked and unashamed, still had trouble forsaking their former ways of life. Just before today's text, Paul chastises them for worrying about pagan food regulations, lunar festivals, idolatrous mysticism, and ascetic practices. And again here in chapter 3 Paul scolds them that though they'd died with Christ they still haven't put to death their prior way of life, their malice, their deception, their fornication.

How does that happen?

They'd risked too much when they'd become Christian not to have felt its truth down deep inside them. But, it didn't stick. They knew that Jesus is Lord; too much was at stake for them not to have taken their faith with life-and-death seriousness. Still, it didn't take. They believed that they'd been set free to live as a new creation. Yet, they fell back to doing what they'd done in the old creation. They had stripped naked for Christ, but they still hadn't put him on. Why not? Or, *how* not?

It's revealing. In chapter 2 Paul admonishes the Colossians against false philosophy, wrong thinking, and deceitful beliefs. In other words, Paul scolds them to get their heads straight, but then his prescription for false thinking and wrong belief is through their hands; through their habits. And then here in chapter 3 it's the very same dynamic. Paul tells them in verse 2 (ESV) to "set your minds on things that are above." But then, further down in verse 12, what Paul commends to them is not beliefs but practices, not ideas but doings. Paul uses a clothing metaphor, "Put on then, as God's chosen ones, holy and beloved, compassionate hearts, kindness, humility, meekness, and patience" (Colossians 3:12 ESV).

Anyone who's been around little kids knows that putting clothes on them takes practice. Compassion, humility, patience—these aren't attitudes in our heads. They're not affections in our hearts. They're virtues. They're moral attributes that you can only acquire over time through habits. Through hands-on practice. We assume our feelings of love for God produce works of love, that faith leads to action. I mean, we make habit a dirty word and suppose that we're saved by the sincerity of our feelings for God or the strength of our belief in God. But for Paul it's our habits that shape our feelings and beliefs. For Paul, the way to our hearts, the way into our heads, is through our hands. Through practices and actions and habits and everyday doings. Before you can invite Jesus in to your heart, before you can conform your mind to Christ, you've got to put him on and practice, which appears to be the very thing the twelve-year-old Jesus does in the temple.

You've got to practice serving the poor so that it becomes a habit until that habit becomes compassion. You've got to practice praising God, week in and week out, until it becomes such a habit that you know without thinking about it that you are a creature of God, which makes you *not* God, which becomes humility. You've got to practice confessing your sins and bringing another's sins to them without malice and passing the peace of Christ until those practices become habits because eventually those habits will make you forgiving. You've got to practice praying "Thy Kingdom come . . ." and working toward that Kingdom in desperate places that defy such hope.

You see, if you do not put on Christ, if you do not practice the habits of Jesus following, then all your other habits will shape you. That's why it's not a bad idea, for example, to give God one day of your week. Because your heart *will* have a lover. And your habits determine who.

Bringing the Text to Life

Delores Hart was an actress in the 1950s and 1960s. She grew up with her grandpa, who was a movie theater projectionist in Chicago. Delores would sit in the dark alcove of her grandpa's movie house watching film after film and dreaming Tinseltown dreams. After high school and college, Delores Hart landed a role as Elvis Presley's love interest in the 1957 film *Loving You*, a role that featured a provocative fifteen-second kiss with Elvis. She starred with Elvis again in *King Creole* in 1958. She followed that up with an award-winning turn on Broadway in the *Pleasure of His Company*.

Delores Hart was the toast of Hollywood. She was compared to Grace Kelly. She was pursued by Elvis Presley and Paul Newman. Her childhood dreams were coming true. She was engaged to a famous LA architect.

But then in 1963 she was in New York promoting her new movie *Come Fly with Me* when something compelled her—called her—to take a one-way cab ride to the Benedictine abbey, Regina Laudis, in Bethlehem, Connecticut, for a retreat. After the retreat, she returned to her red-carpet Hollywood life and society pages engagement but she was overwhelmed by an ache, a sensation of absence.

Emptiness. "I had it all, everything really, but my life wasn't full," she says in the documentary, *God Is the Bigger Elvis.*[5]

So, she quit her acting gigs. She got rid of all her baubles. And she broke off her engagement. She renounced all of her former dreams and joined that Benedictine convent where she is the head prioress today. She put on Christ. She clothed herself in him. What's more remarkable than her story is the documentary filmmakers's re-action to it, their appropriation of it. This is an HBO film, the flagship station for everything postmodern, post-Christian, and radically secular. Here's this odd story of a woman giving up her red-carpet dreams and giving her life to God, and the filmmakers aren't just respectful of her story; they're drawn to it. They're not just interested in her life; they're captivated by her life. Even though it's clear in the film that her motivation—her life in Christ—is a mystery to them, you can tell from the way they film her story that they think, even though she wears a habit and has no husband or family or ordinary aspirations, her life is captivating, that believing she is God's beloved and living fully into that belief has made her life not just captivating but beautiful. You can tell these Hollywood have-it-alls suspect that maybe she is somehow more human than they are. More fully human.

Notes

February

1. John Wesley, journal entry, November 1, 1767, quoted in "All Saints Day: A Holy Day John Wesley Loved," by Joe Lovino, October 28, 2015, https://umc.org/en/content/all-saints-day-a-holy-day-john-wesley-loved.

2. T. S. Eliot, "The Rock," *T. S. Eliot Collected Poems*, 1909–1962, centenary edition (New York: Ecco, 1991), 160.

3. "How Long Will the Famous Be Remembered after Death?" Preaching-Today, February 2019, https://preachingtoday.com/illustrations/2019/february/how-long-will-famous-be-remembered-after-death.html.

4. "How Long Will the Famous Be Remembered after Death?"

5. "Candy Bar Prize No Sweet Reward," CBS News, June 23, 2005, https://cbsnews.com/news/candy-bar-prize-no-sweet-reward/.

6. N. T. Wright, "Grasped by the Love of God," N.T. Wright Online, https://ntwrightonline.org/grasped-love-god/.

March

1. D. T. Niles, *That They May Have Life* (New York: Harper & Brothers, 1951), 96.

2. James Rowe, "Love Lifted Me," 1912, public domain.

April

1. Barbara Brown Taylor, *God in Pain: The Mystery of Suffering* (Nashville: Abingdon, 1998), 80.

2. John Wesley, quoted in *Hymns and Poems* (1739), Duke Center for Studies in the Wesleyan Tradition, ed. Randy L. Maddox, with assistance from Aileen F. Maddox, December 22, 2020.

May

1. William H. Willimon, *Acts*, Interpretation: A Bible Commentary for Teaching and Preaching (Louisville, KY: Westminster John Knox, 1988), 33.

2. John K. Bergland, introduction to *One Heaven of a Party*, Sermons on the First Readings for Lent and Easter Cycle C, by Charles D. Reeb (Lima, OH: CSS Publishing Company, 2003), 10.

3. Joanne Marxhausen, *3-in-1: A Picture of God*, rev. ed. (St. Louis: Concordia Publishing, 2004).

June

1. H. A. Williams, "Tensions," in *A Guide to Prayer for Ministers and Other Servants*, edited by Reuben P. Job and Norman Shawchuck (Nashville, TN: The Upper Room, 1998), 239.

2. "The Story: In the Beginning," *Spill the Beans* 20 (2016): 9, https://www.spillthebeans.org.uk/past-issues.

3. Jon Stole, *The Monster at the End of the Book*, 2nd ed. (New York: Golden Books, 2003).

4. Bernard Brandon Scott, *Hear Then the Parable: A Commentary on the Parables of Jesus* (Minneapolis: Augsburg Fortress, 1989), 380–82.

5. Ronald A. Heifetz and Marty Linsky, *Leadership on the Line: Staying Alive Through the Dangers of Change*, rev. ed. (Cambridge, MA: Harvard Business Review Press, 2017), 7.

6. John Wesley, April 2, 1739 journal entry, *The Journal of John Wesley*, https://www.ccel.org/w/wesley/journal/cache/journal.pdf, 58, accessed September 13, 2022.

7. UMTV: Vital Church Makes Disciples, February 6, 2015, https://www.umc.org/en/content/umtv-vital-church-makes-disciples, accessed September 13, 2022.

8. "A Life-changing Question for a Teen Who Always Ate Lunch Alone," CBS This Morning, November 15, 2018, https://www.youtube.com/watch?v=d6aXXIiIkLc, accessed September 13, 2022.

August

1. N. T. Wright, *Simply Christian: Why Christianity Makes Sense* (New York: Harper Collins, 2006), 33.

2. James A. Harnish, Passion, *Power & Praise: A Model for Men's Spirituality from the Life of David* (Nashville, TN: Abingdon Press, 2000), 149.

September

1. *NRSV Wesley Study Bible*, s.v. "James 1:19-27" (Nashville, TN: Abingdon Press, 2009), 1500.

2. John F. A. Sawyer, "Isaiah 35:1-10," *The Daily Study Bible: Old Testament* (Louisville, KY: Westminster/John Knox Press, 1986), 17–18.

3. Oliver Darcy, "Seth Rich Conspiracy Theorists Retract and Apologize for False Statements as They Settle Lawsuit," CNN Business, January 14, 2021, https://www.cnn.com/2021/01/14/media/seth-rich-lawsuit-settlement-ed-butowsky/index.html.

4. Shannon Bond, "How Alex Jones Helped Mainstream Conspiracy Theories Become Part of American Life," Weekend Edition Saturday, NPR, August 6, 2022, https://www.npr.org/2022/08/06/1115936712/how-alex-jones-helped-mainstream-conspiracy-theories-into-american-life.

5. Rick Bragg, "Oseola McCarty, a Washerwoman Who Gave All She Had to Help Others, Dies at 91," *New York Times*, September 28, 1999.

6. Colleen Cheslak, "Hedy Lamarr (1914–2000)," National Women's History Museum, https://www.womenshistory.org/education-resources/biographies/hedy-lamarr.

October

1. Lauren Soth, "Van Gogh's Agony," *The Art Bulletin*, Vol. 68, No. 2 (Jun. 1986), 309.

2. From Hemingway's letter to his father in 1925, *Ernest Hemingway: Selected Letters 1917–1961*, ed. Carlos Baker (New York: Scribner, 2003), 153.

November

1. Gerard Stephen Sloan, *John*, Interpretation (Atlanta: John Knox Press, 1988), 144.

2. J. Wallace Hamilton, "Make a Friend of Your Fear!" in *Ride the Wild Horses! The Christian Use of Our Untamed Impulses* (Old Tappan, NJ: Fleming H. Revell Company, 1952), 109.

3. https://www.treatsforthesoul.org/wednesday-worry-box/.

December

1. https://www.europelanguagejobs.com/blog/turning_advent_into_adventure.php.

2. Barbara Brown Taylor, "Surprised by Joy," *The Living Pulpit* (October-December, 1996), 16.

3. Martin Luther, *Luther's Works: Lectures on Titus, Philemon, and Hebrews*, edited by Hilton C. Oswald and Helmut T. Lehmann (St. Louis: Concordia, 1955), 65.

4. Martin Luther, "A Brief Instruction on What to Look for and Expect in the Gospels," *Martin Luther's Basic Theological Writings*, edited by William R. Russell, Timothy F. Lull (Minneapolis: Fortress, 2012), ch. 9.

5. *God Is the Bigger Elvis*, directed by Rebecca Cammissa (Hudson Yards, NY: HBO, 2011).

Contributors

Sam Parkes—Pastor, Mary Esther United Methodist Church, Mary Esther, Florida

Laurie Moeller—Senior Pastor, Northbrook United Methodist Church, Roswell, Georgia

Chris Jones—Senior Pastor, Asbury United Methodist Church, Maitland, Florida

Jasmine Rose Smothers—Lead Pastor, Atlanta First United Methodist Church, Atlanta, Georgia

Will Willimon—Retired Bishop of the United Methodist Church and Professor of the Practice of Christian Ministry, Duke Divinity School, Durham, North Carolina

Alex Shanks—Assistant to the Bishop, The Florida Conference of the UMC, Lakeland, Florida

Robin C. Wilson—Pastor, First United Methodist Church of Phenix City, Phenix, City, Alabama

Charley Reeb—General Editor, Abingdon Preaching Annual and Senior Pastor of Johns Creek United Methodist Church, Johns Creek, Georgia

Lynn Bartlow—Lead Pastor, St. Mark's United Methodist Church, Tucson, Arizona

Cyndi McDonald—Senior Pastor, McKendree United Methodist Church, Barnesville, Georgia

Vidalis Lopez—First United Methodist Church of Coral Springs, Coral Springs, Florida

Cynthia D. Weems—Superintendent of the South East District of the Florida Conference of the United Methodist Church

Jennifer Forrester—Associate Pastor, First United Methodist Church of Hickory, Hickory, North Carolina

Beth LaRocca Pitts—Pastor, Oak Grove United Methodist Church, Decatur, Georgia

Will Zant—Pastor, Haygood Memorial United Methodist Church, Atlanta, Georgia

Paul Christy—Senior Pastor, First United Methodist Church of Hickory, Hickory, North Carolina

Ron Bartlow—Senior Pastor, St. Paul's United Methodist Church, Tucson, Arizona

Jim Somerville—Senior Pastor, First Baptist Church of Richmond, Virginia

Jason Micheli—Head Pastor, Annandale United Methodist Church, Annandale, Virginia

Scripture Index

Old Testament

New Testament

The Apocrypha

Thematic Index

Online Edition

The Abingdon Preaching Annual 2024 online edition is available by subscription at www.ministrymatters.com.

Abingdon Press is pleased to make available an online edition of *The Abingdon Preaching Annual 2024* as part of our Ministry Matters online community and resources.

Subscribers to our online edition will also have access to preaching content from prior years.

Visit www.ministrymatters.com and click on SUBSCRIBE NOW. From that menu, select "Abingdon Preaching Annual" and follow the prompt to set up an account.

Please note, your subscription to the Abingdon Preaching Annual will be renewed automatically, unless you contact MinistryMatters.com to request a change.